T0320018

Corporate Venturing

Corporate Venturing

ORGANIZING FOR INNOVATION

Jessica van den Bosch
Tilburg Center of Entrepreneurship (TCE), Tilburg University, The Netherlands

Geert Duysters
Tilburg Center of Entrepreneurship (TCE), Tilburg University, The Netherlands

Edward Elgar
Cheltenham, UK • Northampton, MA, USA

Published by
Edward Elgar Publishing Limited
The Lypiatts
15 Lansdown Road
Cheltenham
Glos GL50 2JA
UK

Edward Elgar Publishing, Inc.
William Pratt House
9 Dewey Court
Northampton
Massachusetts 01060
USA

A catalogue record for this book
is available from the British Library

Library of Congress Control Number: 2014938831

This book is available electronically in the ElgarOnline.com Business Subject Collection, E-ISBN 978 1 78347 660 2

ISBN 978 1 78347 659 6 (cased)

Typeset by Servis Filmsetting Ltd, Stockport, Cheshire
Printed and bound in Great Britain by T.J. International Ltd, Padstow

Contents in brief

Full contents

Main authors and contributors

Main authors

Jessica van den Bosch is managing director of the Tilburg Center of Entrepreneurship and a fellow of the Corporate Entrepreneurship Research Center, both located at Tilburg University in the Netherlands. Jessica studied law at Leiden University and has an MBA from Keele University (UK). Jessica is interested in the combination of management dynamics, professional practice and corporate entrepreneurship.

Geert Duysters is a full professor of entrepreneurship and innovation at Tilburg University. He acts as the scientific director of the Tilburg Center of Entrepreneurship. His academic research mainly concerns innovation strategies, mergers and acquisitions, corporate entrepreneurship and strategic alliances. He has published over 100 international refereed articles and six books on corporate innovation.

Contributors

Arjan van den Born is professor of entrepreneurship and creativity at Tilburg University. He acts as the director of the Creativity Entrepreneurship Lab. His academic research mainly concerns entrepreneurship, creativity, networks, communities and organizational change. He has published various international refereed articles and various books.

Victor Gilsing is a full professor of corporate innovation and entrepreneurship at University of Antwerp (Prinsstraat 13, 2000 Antwerpen) and Tilburg University. He acts as the co-leader of ACED, a research institute for organization and innovation at Antwerp University, and is also one of the core fellows of the Center for Innovation Research at Tilburg University. He has published in various top academic journals, such as *Journal of Management*, *Journal of Management Studies*, *Research Policy*, *Technovation* and others. Furthermore, he regularly teaches for senior executives, CFOs and both corporate and independent venture managers.

Stijn van den Hoogen lectures on entrepreneurship and strategic management at Tilburg University. He is working on his PhD on the topic of corporate venturing, which is also his main research area.

Preface

Over the past decades we have witnessed a growing number of companies that are unable to deal with their rapidly changing business and technological environments. Once-leading companies, such as Kodak, Nokia and Digital Equipment Corporation, have given way to new firms riding the waves of new technologies. Today even entire industries have become the victims of the forces of 'creative destruction' arising from the emergence of the internet, new technologies and new business models (e.g., low-cost airlines). Video stores, PC makers and bricks-and-mortar travel agencies have become the dinosaurs of our time.

Moreover, the speed of technological and market change has exploded recently due to fast-paced innovations in technology, shrinking product and technology life cycles, the changing role of consumers and ongoing globalization. Large firms, in particular, are struggling to keep up with these changes, which render existing skills and know-how useless within short periods of time. Their continuous investment in equipment, people and existing markets makes it very costly for them to quickly switch to new markets or benefit from new windows of opportunities. Incumbent firms are typically inert, bureaucratic and resistant to change (rather than embracing it). Their core competencies have started transforming into core rigidities, prohibiting them from benefiting from new opportunities. New firms, on the other hand, do not suffer from market myopia or business inertia. They are the ones that open up new markets and reap the benefits of changing technologies, markets and consumer preferences. However, these small firms obviously lack the marked advantages of large firms in terms of branding, efficiency, supply networks and finance.

The ideal corporation, therefore, is able to combine the scale and pure power of a large organization with the creativity, flexibility and resilience of a small one. As a result, some large firms gradually started over time to embrace new ways of dealing with these changing environments. Through strategic alliances, minority holdings and mergers and acquisitions, incumbent firms started expanding the boundaries of their organizations in a desperate effort to increase their flexibility and resilience (Chesbrough, 2003). Apart from these new modes of organization, firms are increasingly experimenting with new organizational forms more closely aligned with the true entrepreneurial traits of small start-up organizations.

One of the most promising new developments in this line of endeavours is that of investing in corporate venturing. Corporate venturing can be described as the process of creating new ventures within large organizations. There are various ways of organizing this process. One way is to create internal funds that enable the corporate to invest in small, external, innovative start-ups; another is to establish an internal business unit dedicated to creating innovative start-ups. The former method of investing in innovation is more financially focussed, while the latter form of venture organization aims to benefit from the entrepreneurial spirit of such start-ups without the burden of the parent company's bureaucracy.

Both forms are in vogue lately as more and more firms realize that to beat the forces of disruption they must peg their survival on bringing entrepreneurship into the boundaries of their large corporations. In 2011 as much as 11 per cent of all venture capital invested in the USA was provided by corporate funds (Lerner, 2013). In a similar vein, an increasing number of firms are setting up new business units dedicated to creating new start-ups within the boundaries of the parent firm. Typically, an internal budget will be created for investing in new ideas that could potentially transform the company's main line of business. The role of the parent company is to assist with financing, technology and marketing, but it must be careful not to interfere too much, so as to preserve the entrepreneurial spirit of the venturing unit. There is a clear danger of being either under- or over-involved as a parent.

Because of a lack of tradition in this field of venturing, firms are constantly searching for more information on how to manage corporate ventures. Best practices are almost completely lacking and the contemporary literature on corporate venturing is not very extensive (what there is tends to treat the venturing process as a black box). There is certainly not a strong body of literature on the management of corporate ventures. This is striking given that recent research suggests that only 5 per cent of corporate venturing units manage to create new substantial lines of business for their parent companies (Birkinshaw and Campbell, 2004) and the median life span of a corporate venturing investment is only about one year (Lerner, 2013). With such a low success rate, it seems vital to create more insight into how to manage ventures successfully. We need to gain a greater understanding of both the process and management of ventures by looking into the black box of corporate venturing.

In this book we aim to take the first step to that end by sharing real-world best practices from a number of different business settings, ranging from health insurance and newspapers to universities and the food industry. Despite the differences, we have been able to spot some common business practices and shared potential pitfalls. Each case is organized around a common theme, reflecting on four operational elements. The case studies tell the honest stories of the creators of the ventures, who reveal their failures and successes, their struggles, their problems and their solutions. These corporate entrepreneurs open up the black box of their ventures and unveil their key insights into the secrets of successful venturing.

By interviewing the corporate venture directors, managers and CFOs of eight organizations, we acquired interesting and relevant insights into the venturing process. These interviews formed the groundwork for a unique set of detailed cases that provide a real-life vision of how corporate venture organizations are managed in practice. By subsequently analysing these cases, we aim to derive relevant guidelines and lessons learned. This sets us up for a more detailed and better understanding of the key success factors in corporate venturing.

As described above, organizations are often not very capable of organizing more radical innovation internally. And as Schumpeter discussed in the 1930s many of the most important innovations come about by *new* combinations of technologies (Schumpeter, 1939). This requires firms to broaden their scope and open up their innovation process to benefit from innovations developed outside their organization. Corporate venturing is often seen as a panacea for the 'not-invented-here syndrome' that is characteristic of many firms and their respective internal R&D departments. However, venturing requires a continuous balance between efficiency and creativity, corporate objectives and venture team objectives, funds allocated to the internal R&D department and those allocated to the venture, and so on. Venture management is inherently difficult and requires a delicate management approach.

In this book we introduce four operational elements that are found to be instrumental in building a successful venturing organization:

Model

The first operational element firms need to consider is the fact that innovation units require a different form of organizational support from the parent company. They need more flexibility and the freedom to move away from corporate bureaucracy and handle things differently. This requires a *model* that offers them that creative space on the one hand, while focussing on the effective execution of their mission on the other. Through the use of models, documents and forms, firms can create a clear, organization-wide understanding of how certain things should be handled, how certain actions should be implemented and how issues should be solved. Processes are generally considered to improve efficiency in an organization, but they can at the same time kill any entrepreneurial or creative spirit.

Stage-gate models, such as illustrated in Figure P.1, are widely embraced in venturing. The process is funnel-shaped in that at every stage a selection process takes place and some projects might be terminated. Each stage ends with a go/no-go moment, a point at which an investment committee (often) decides whether the venture should enter the next stage or not – whether it needs more work and research done or should be killed. Admission to the next stage implies making a larger investment than was required at the previous stage, both in the terms of financing and the time and dedication of the venture manager. The level of investment is often seen to be increasing exponentially over time. The investment committee often consists of the parent company's senior management, preferably from various business units. Another important condition is multidisciplinarity, since most innovations arise at the interface of two disciplines.

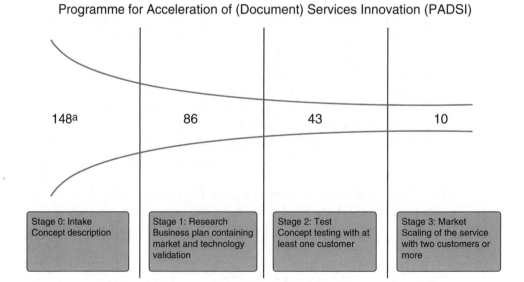

Programme for Acceleration of (Document) Services Innovation (PADSI)

|148a|86|43|10|

| Stage 0: Intake Concept description | Stage 1: Research Business plan containing market and technology validation | Stage 2: Test Concept testing with at least one customer | Stage 3: Market Scaling of the service with two customers or more |

Note: a. Cumulative number of companies involved in the Programme. The other figures are numbers of companies involved at each stage.

Figure P.1 Funnel-shaped Document Services Valley (DSV) stage-gate process

Portfolio

The second operational element is that innovation units need to be able to retain a different focus than that of the parent company. Their aim is to come up with new business ideas that are in line with the parent company's strategic vision but should also deviate from the core business. It is therefore considered essential to have a clearly defined *portfolio*, which maximizes synergy with the parent but at the same time generates new businesses. As we will see from the cases presented, a well-balanced portfolio is key to providing corporate alignment, risk management and focus.

Staffing the team

The third element is that innovation units require a specific kind of combination of human talent since the skills necessary for realizing innovation are different from those needed for performing core business activities. Creativity, entrepreneurship, perseverance and political skills are just some examples of the skills needed in *teams* that are working on new business ideas.

Current literature defines three levels of innovation: core innovation, adjacent innovation and transformational innovation. Core innovation involves companies that are optimizing their existing products for existing markets, while transformational innovation is about creating new products for new markets. Adjacent innovation is positioned in between these two forms of innovation and requires expanding the existing business to 'new-to-the-company' business (Nagji and Tuff, 2012).

For transformational innovation one needs skills other than for core innovation or adjacent innovation. So how do you find the people with the transformational skills in order to get them involved in your innovation unit? The great advantage of venture organizations is that they attract entrepreneurially minded people who have many of the skills and attributes needed to work in a creative setting. Getting the right people in the bus and in the right seats is key to successful venturing. However, these people need to be capable of connecting with corporate management in terms of realizing synergies.

Integration

Integration is the fourth element. The aim of venturing is to realize new business that should be able to be integrated successfully into the parent company in due time (otherwise why bother?). This requires a vision of how new business is *related* to the *parent company*. When a corporate decides to start venturing, it needs to be aware of the fact that venture units need a certain amount of freedom in order to be entrepreneurial. The bureaucracy of the parent company often impedes a venture unit in realizing its goals since the venture needs flexibility and not efficiency to live by. On the other hand, when a venture unit has successfully realized a product or technology that is of value to the parent company, there comes a time when that venture needs to be integrated ('spun in') into the parent company. In order to integrate successfully, venture directors need to think about how they will eventually organize the integration long before it actually has to happen.

In the following chapters we discuss eight individual cases: CbusineZ, AkzoNobel, BAC (Unilever), DSV (Océ Canon), Rabobank, Eindhoven University of Technology's InnovationLab, Sanoma and *nrc·next*. In Chapter 9 we will discuss the outcomes of the various cases and present our conclusions, followed in Chapter 10 by our top ten best practices for managing corporate ventures.

This book aims to inform venture management, entrepreneurship scholars and corporate management about the challenges, opportunities, risks and day-to-day management of corporate ventures. We therefore explore the whole venture cycle, all the way from the initial start-up to the day-to-day operations or exit. This provides a unique insight into the venturing process as seen from the personal perspective of venture experts, venture managers and corporate staff.

Acknowledgements

We would like to thank all the people who contributed to this book by discussing their cases with us. A special thanks to Martijn Houtkamp, Robin van Rossum and Nina Woodson. We hope you enjoy reading this book as much as we did writing it.

Jessica van den Bosch
Geert Duysters

1

Corporate venturing in health care: a CbusineZ case

Jessica van den Bosch and Geert Duysters

'To develop innovations that help solve specific problems in health care'. That was the reason CbusineZ was founded in 2001, in the words of Joep de Groot, Chairman of the Board of Directors. CbusineZ saw opportunities in areas where the standard measures employed by its parent company, the health insurance company CZ Zorgverzekeringen, might fail to produce the desired results.

The company was launched ten years ago with only a director and a secretary and now has a team of 15 employees. Originally financed with a €10 million loan from CZ, CbusineZ is now largely financially independent. Sales are encouraging and CbusineZ's ventures yield sufficient resources for funding a substantial share of the investments being made.

Parent and subsidiary

CZ is a not-for-profit mutual benefit company that insures 3.5 million subscribers. The company operates under several names besides CZ, including Delta Lloyd and OHRA, and controls about 20 per cent of the market in total. CZ has approximately 2500 employees working at its locations in Breda, Goes, Sittard and Tilburg and in various service offices. Annual turnover is of the order of over €7 billion. It holds several labels and all products and/or services are developed for CZ as a whole. Figure 1.1 illustrates the structure of CZ.

As part of its vision, CZ wants to improve health care services and keep them affordable. In 2012 this challenge was also at the top of the social agenda in the Netherlands, with the ageing population and rising health care costs as major contributing factors. CZ has been seeking innovative ways to keep health care affordable for years. In fact, CbusineZ was established back in 2001. It is CZ's health care innovation and venture capital company. The company is a separate legal entity from its parent company, CZ, with its own Board of Directors and Supervisory Board. There is some crossover though in that the chair of the CZ Supervisory Board is also appointed as chair of the CbusineZ Supervisory Board.

CbusineZ facilitates health care innovation by acting as an incubator to start up new initiatives or by participating in existing ones. Most of these initiatives tackle bottleneck issues in health care that tend not to be addressed because the investments needed are relatively high or the pay-back period too long. Sometimes the underlying problem is political or the issues are difficult to address because they require bringing together very specific types of knowledge and expertise. CbusineZ tackles these bottlenecks from a strategic vantage point, believing that solving them will help achieve strategic objec-

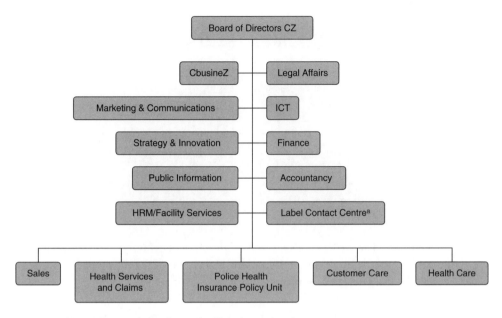

Note: a. Customer help call centre for CZ products and services.

Figure 1.1 CZ structure

tives over the long term, such as lowering health care costs, improving quality of care and effecting lifestyle change. There is also profit to be gained in the fact that these initiatives improve the supply strategy of parent company CZ.

'We tackle these kinds of issues, generate new ideas, launch a separate venture to develop them and try to organize it in such a way that the strategic value is realized. That's what it's all about', says De Groot. In other words, the venturing revolves around achieving strategic and financial objectives. Figure 1.2 shows how CbusineZ is structured.

New ventures at CbusineZ are mostly dedicated to supporting or further professionalizing the activities of parent organization CZ. A new venture should help purchasers improve purchasing processes and provide clients with more choice. Some CbusineZ ventures are started because CZ has been unable to take up a particular issue due to lack of time or focus. One good example is online treatment in the area of mental health services. De Groot explains:

> Everyone knows this approach has been effective for at least ten years, but they still don't adopt it because of purchasing policies. Then it feels good to work with other parties to form a joint venture and involve the purchasing team in its design and development. It helps our clients and lowers health care costs.

Figure 1.2 CbusineZ
structure

That was the birth of Psy Health Direct, a venture that provides mental health care through online treatment and is one of the newest developments in e-health (health care provided through the internet).

Many of the innovations CbusineZ pursues can only be realized by working together with other parties. 'Almost all of our ventures are joint ventures', says De Groot. Because the CbusineZ ventures rarely concern new products per se and are primarily aimed at developing new services, the term 'innovation' can sometimes be misleading. While there are very few truly pioneering innovations even in the product sector, innovation in the service sector consists primarily of developing and applying new processes or business models, such as new working practices that yield savings or reach different target groups. 'Take the formation of a venture that performs national benchmark research. Novel? No. Innovative? Within the health care sector, yes', De Groot points out.

Caring about health care

Although one of the essential reasons for CbusineZ's formation was purchasing management, the company's overall vision is founded on social conviction: literally 'caring about health care'. In the next ten years, the number of people in the Netherlands suffering from diabetes and heart failure will reach 1.2 million and 1.1 million respectively (Figure 1.3). Health care costs are rising at an annual rate of 8–9 per cent.

The present Dutch health care system is not sustainable. It lacks transparency and the processes are not rational – more importantly they are not clearly monitored. In addition there is a shortage of personnel. 'Any attempts to improve the sector must include modernizing it', proclaims De Groot. 'The

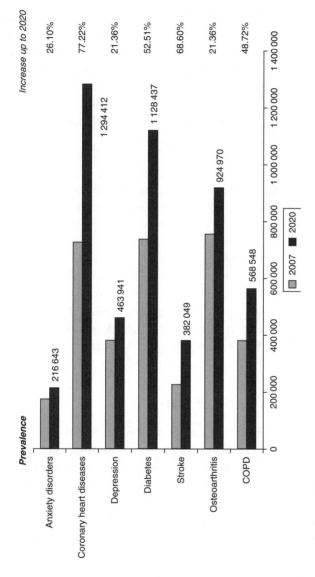

Source: Landelijk Informatie Netwerk Huisartsenzorg (LINH) and Rijksinstituut voor Volksgezondheid en Milieu (RIVM).

Figure 1.3 Increase in chronic diseases from 2007 to 2020

business world has a natural tendency toward innovation; otherwise, at some point, you simply go out of business. This is not true with regard to the health care sector. Health care institutions will not pursue innovation on their own if no one around them spurs them on'.

The fact that market dynamics are increasingly relevant in health care has influenced the corporate venturing undertaken by CZ. Improving the balance between supply and demand should result in better customer service, and a better supply strategy will also result in more affordable health care. All of that was reason enough for De Groot and his team to go into venturing: entrepreneurial activities in which new businesses are created and owned by the corporation together with one or more external partners.

CbusineZ concentrates on collaborative corporate venturing. Anything that does not fall into this category is rejected or referred to the parent company, CZ. Of course, such things are not always so cut and dried. There is often a grey area when CbusineZ works together with its parent company and outside parties; then it can be tricky to determine if the endeavour is a partnership or a venture. In such cases, they explore whether it should be set up as a separate venture. These kinds of projects fall under the responsibility of CbusineZ. The innovative projects that are more aligned with traditional purchasing matters – or that do not involve any other partners – fall under the auspices of the Health Care Innovation Department at CZ. This department takes a different, more traditional approach, in which budgets and controllability are decisive factors. CbusineZ takes a more entrepreneurial approach and looks at the viability of an innovative idea.

The venture process at CbusineZ

Setting up a separate venture might sound easier than it really is. Establishing a start-up is a step-by-step process. Step one involves evaluating the opportunities. If the evaluation is sufficiently positive, then you move on to making a business plan. In cases involving a strategic partner, the partners put forward a budget, in which each party assumes an equal share of the costs, even though the new business has yet to take shape. As soon as that plan is completed, the parties look more closely at budgeting, organizational form and arranging funding.

'The financing is often done in blocks', explains De Groot:

> If nothing else, this forces the future venture manager to become accustomed to
> insufficient liquidity. All of our people come from backgrounds where they are

used to having adequate financial resources. They are not accustomed to having to scrimp. Even with limited budgets, there is always some room. But in this case, the venture manager receives a block of financing in the company's bank account, and once that money's gone, he or she has a problem. That makes them smarter in their financial planning.

The financial constructions underlying the ventures can vary considerably. Sometimes CbusineZ enters into a joint venture that involves share ownership, whereas in other cases intellectual property is sold under a profit-sharing agreement. All of the financing is divided up into portions and rigorously orchestrated. This includes the revenues; the private limited companies pay these to CbusineZ as soon as the proceeds exceed a predefined solvency limit. That payment is earmarked for investing in new initiatives. Another thing to always keep in mind is the risk of a private limited company having too much money. Then there's a chance that the venture will 'play around' with that money, which is not the idea.

CbusineZ is leading the way in terms of corporate venturing in the health care sector. Ten years ago, CZ was the first health care operator, along with one other insurer, to enter into venturing. Now other insurers have joined in. CbusineZ has expanded its lead in the past year by further professionalizing. This prompted a big market demand for advice. 'We put a great deal of time into this', says De Groot:

> In sector ventures we will often make a director available. The unwritten rule is that
> the search for a director is open, but in practice we generally provide the director.
> The advantage to that is that it makes it somewhat easier to manage our own
> strategic value. That is, indeed, what we do and we take it seriously.

Psy Health Direct: a business case

It is obvious these days that the internet offers opportunities for mental health care. Scientific research has demonstrated that enabling online treatment of depression and anxiety, for instance, could be very effective. Additional market research, moreover, shows that 40 per cent of those surveyed would want to receive treatment for depression online, whereas only 1 per cent were eventually offered it as an option. So, there appears to be a great deal of demand for such a product but little supply: an excellent opportunity.

CbusineZ was approached by Interhealth, which was working on providing online treatment but had not yet been successful. The proposal was to join forces in coordinated action to make this project a success. That was the start of what was later called Psy Health Direct. It started with a preliminary study using the CbusineZ Venturing Model (CVM – see Figure 1.6 below). This yielded some interesting information. For one thing, the purchasing policy of parent organization CZ had no provisions for using the internet for mental health care – for a sector, it is worth noting, with annual costs in the order of €6 billion. This e-health venture, therefore, fitted in the portfolio perfectly, from both a self-management and a cost-reduction standpoint.

It promised benefits for purchasers of health care, as well. Many people who suffer from burn-out are referred to a psychologist by their HRM department and company doctor. This is a very costly process. But these people too can be helped through less expensive measures. The treatment method also opens the possibility of allowing people to continue working while they receive treatment at home. Moreover, internet treatment can be used for prevention as well.

Based on all this information it was decided to consider the business market as the target group. Absenteeism costs companies €2500 per patient in treatment. Treatment through first-line providers (psychologists) costs about €640; second-line treatment (the former RIAGGs, or outpatient mental health care institutes) runs to about €1200. With Psy Health Direct, comparable treatment through the internet would amount to €400 per patient treated – a considerable saving.

The connection with CZ in this case involved the fact that CZ would have to change its purchasing policy to encourage online treatment. Organizations should be allowed to build in higher margins for online treatment, for example. (The profit margins on standard treatment are capped.) This approach would have to apply to all types of online treatment, not just those offered by Psy Health Direct.

Based on the market research, the decision was taken to further develop the venture together with Interhealth. The primary issues to be addressed involved the organizational structure and how to deal with the company and its accumulated losses. This culminated in a participation agreement. At the same time that this was being arranged, a parallel process was exploring the best way to configure the purchasing side. These two processes then came together in a joint venture agreement. 'It was interesting to see how Interhealth approached things from the product and technology side', says De Groot. 'We thought about things from the perspective of the market and expected growth'.

In the end they chose to focus on the business market: companies that purchase health care for employees suffering from burn-out or depression, for example. At first glance this is not where the strategic value necessarily was for CZ. Its interests lay more in the area of first- and second-line health care services. 'But you have to have sufficient volume', De Groot explains:

> You can devote all your resources to pushing the second-line care – because that's where the big money is – but the pace of adoption is too slow. For the venture to be viable, we have to actually get the business market on board first. Then you are generating cash flows. After that you can start investing in the first- and second-line services. That's where we're at now.

There was a fringe benefit to implementing the venture, discovered in the two options that the product developed afforded for first-line care; in addition to the product itself, the sale of licences turned out to be an interesting opportunity. Due to a drop in the number of treatments covered – from eight to five – use of this product became particularly interesting for the first-line care target group. The loss in turnover could be compensated by using the new online treatments to treat more people.

For the health care insurers, including CZ, it was an interesting development. Successful first-line treatment results in fewer people having to resort to a second line of treatment. This care programme achieved innovation by focusing on the savings generated by the product and curbing costs by decreasing the number of treatments covered. 'That kind of financial trigger has worked for years in the business world', De Groot points out, 'and it works here, too. People will innovate if they have to'.

But does all this really help the consumer? You would expect treatment to be more effective when the patient and counsellor can actually see and talk to one another and there is a level of physical attention and prodding to be proactive. To what extent does online care and treatment really contribute to recovery?

'Without monitoring, e-health doesn't work so well', De Groot admits:

> What we offer with Psy Health Direct is a counselling programme that starts with a consultation, followed by several sessions using the internet program. Then the client is called back. That way we can establish a rhythm. According to the literature, the impact of counselling supervision comes primarily from the motivational influence. The internet program triggers a 'click' in the patient when he or she has completed certain exercises. The most important thing is having that

motivation from other people to persevere with the treatment. And we create that through human contact.

Applying that combination in this form of treatment boosts efficiency. And that makes a world of difference to not only the health care insurer's Purchasing department, but also the subscriber. This method of treatment is attractive for the latter because it reduces the amount they have to contribute themselves. And that helps encourage the use of e-health over today's standard treatments.

Evolution

The venture got off to an auspicious start. The participation was settled; the funding was secured; and the location was assigned. The next step involved staffing. A director was appointed from CbusineZ to work alongside the director from Interhealth. The two directors teamed up and got down to business launching the venture. With the support of an experienced psychologist, a business manager from CbusineZ and a consultant, the work process was thought out in greater detail with the aim of ultimately developing the product and a marketing plan, among other things. Three months later, it became apparent that, despite the development efforts, the product could not go live. All of the facilities had been secured and a team was standing by, ready to get to work. The case landed in a red folder on De Groot's desk. What was going on?

The stages of the CbusineZ Venturing Model (CVM) had been followed throughout the process and the product fitted nicely into the portfolio. And yet the venture did not get off the ground. What could that be attributed to? In hindsight, one can conclude that the CVM model had not been optimally used. 'Yes, the stages were followed, but the stage-specific checklists had not been followed. As a result, the project's progress was not being monitored closely enough', says De Groot.

Another issue was that the two directors working together were unable to take the venture from the design to the implementation stage. They failed to direct the work of the other team members adequately and were afraid to make decisions. At the implementation stage, especially, it is critical that decisions be made about structuring the process. These directors were stalled at the business plan stage. The project was stranded because of both a failure to strictly apply the model and the operational element of staffing.

'It was an unusual experience for me to have to take over like that', declares De Groot. 'I replaced the director who was responsible for operations. We sent the director who was responsible for the technical side of things back to overseeing those details and we appointed a new director alongside him, who was more capable of implementation'.

De Groot approached Angelique Bonte in early February 2012 and asked her if she would take charge of the Psy Health Direct venture as operational director. Bonte accepted the challenge and started by investigating the situation. She quickly discovered that confidence in the venture was sharply eroding at several divisions of the parent company CZ. That lack of confidence stemmed from the fact that, after a full seven months, it had not yet received a clear description of the services being developed and, moreover, the costs being quoted were constantly changing.

'I grabbed the CVM model and went through all of the questions in it, step by step, to put the abundance of information in order and get an understanding of where we should start', says Bonte. In the process, it became clear to her that the proposition had not been concretely enough defined and that the supply processes were unclear. 'On top of that, I started holding meetings with all of the stakeholders to win back their confidence', she continues. 'With the help of De Groot and the shareholders, it worked'.

By getting immediately to work on detailing the proposition and taking command of the marketing, she quickly reintroduced momentum in the venture. By March 2012 the service was launched, though even at that point there were certain matters that still needed to be resolved or improved. 'I realized that the controls were not yet a hundred per cent. As soon as we tackled one thing, a new problem would often pop up', Bonte says.

The venture has had a good start-up in the intervening months and they are working on the expansion stage. The prospects are promising and the organization runs smoothly. 'The hardest thing with a venture that has stranded is to gain insight as quickly as possible, so you can decide where to start', Bonte says. 'You are flooded with information in those early days. The CVM model was extremely helpful in terms of structuring all that information and setting priorities. Now it's just a question of stepping on the gas and going for it'.

'In hindsight we should've known', De Groot says. 'The team lacked a good balance between thinkers and doers. So, in the end, pulling the plug and replacing part of the management team was my responsibility'. The CVM outlines the steps from the business plan stage through the start-up stage to the expansion stage. Since this project stalled at the business plan stage, people should have looked at what elements from the CVM were not working. But they failed to do that, in part because of the make up of the team. The stagnation had nothing to do with the coordination with the parent company; that component did not come into play in this case.

It sometimes happens that ventures stagnate at the start-up stage and a decision is made to end the venture and take it no further. That could have been the case with Psy Health Direct if Bonte had not stepped in to straighten things out. But there can also be extraneous reasons for ending a venture, such as when the market position turns out to be less positive than previously estimated, perhaps due to impediments that were originally overlooked or a new development intersecting the venture and affecting its chances. In such cases, the market might not materialize, so it makes little sense to proceed with the venture.

In the services sector, poorly functioning ventures generally tend to sink to the bottom fairly quickly. That is why, according to De Groot, there are hardly ever any actual failures. With technology ventures it is more common for it to be all or nothing. 'The upswing following the start-up stage is much greater. In services, you can start earning a profit more quickly and easily, but the scaling up is also less pronounced', he explains.

Four operational elements in the venture process

We will be looking at four dynamics that influence the venturing process for this organization. What models does CbusineZ put into practice and how does it do so? A second consideration is portfolio classification, because it provides insight into whether the venturing organization has a particular focus and, if so, on what components. Portfolios provide a method for steering ventures, with the question being whether and how CbusineZ uses them. Staffing at the ventures is the third element. How can you determine whether someone is suited to running a venture? What kinds of skills and knowledge should they possess? What other human aspects affect a venture's success? Finally, we look at how the venturing organization is positioned with regard to the parent company. How is it structured? Where do the venture and the parent company converge and where do they diverge – and why?

CVM: CbusineZ Venturing Model

A typical venture goes through a number of stages. These are illustrated in Figure 1.4.

Every venturing project starts with the idea generation stage. Idea evaluation is about exploring the possibilities and applications; from there one can work

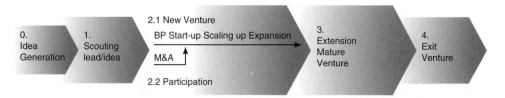

Figure 1.4 CbusineZ venture stages

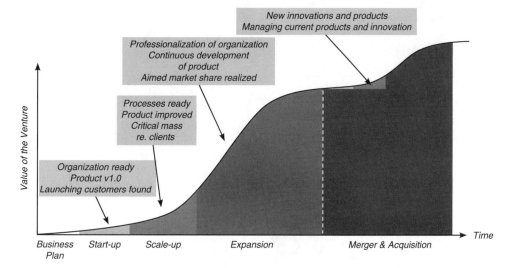

Figure 1.5 Strategic aims and incremental change in value

toward starting the venture (Stage 1). At the next stage, the business plan is used as a basis for moving from the start-up to scaling up operations and expansion (Stage 2). That stage grows into further development of the mature venture (Stage 3) and toward a possible exit plan (Stage 4), as shown in Figure 1.4.

The value of new ventures grows incrementally as shown in Figure 1.5. There is a different focus at each stage. The basic model outlined above can be used at each stage to determine whether a venture is in good shape. Predefined rules for each stage are used to establish whether people and processes are on target and ready to enter the next stage. This general model was modified to incorporate rules specifically designed for the CbusineZ venturing organiza-tion, creating the so-called CVM (see Figure 1.6).

The greatest advantage of this tailor-made model is the ability to focus on where the organization's resources are needed and what the chances of

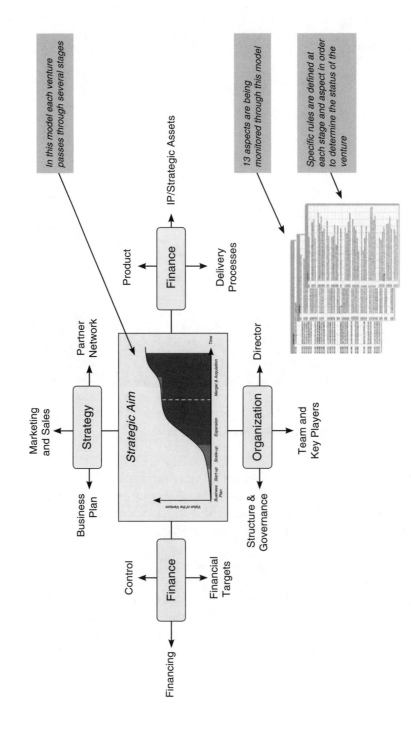

Figure 1.6 CbusineZ Venturing Model

success are. This prevents wasting valuable resources on ventures that turn out to have less promise and be less of a match with the portfolio than originally thought.

Ideas at CbusineZ are generated with the help of both in-house and outside parties. CbusineZ venture managers routinely sit down with innovators to brainstorm and come up with new ideas. Colleagues at the parent organization – especially from the purchasing groups – are also asked on a regular basis about their needs and any ideas they might have. All of these ideas end up on a lead list. The Board of Directors then selects which ideas are worth exploring. 'If we have generated an idea and think it's interesting enough to explore, we also have to have a sense of whether it fits within the portfolio', De Groot explains:

> We ask ourselves whether it needs CbusineZ. If the answer is yes, then we proceed to the evaluation stage. At that stage, we examine the market, hold high-calibre discussions and look into possible organizational structures. Once all of that is worked out, you enter the stage that includes having the Board of Directors decide whether it's a good idea or not, whether it's innovative enough and whether there's a market for it. We also look thoroughly into the technical feasibility. In the end though it comes down to the question of whether it will truly improve health care. So, that's a whole list of criteria that must be formally met before the business plan is drawn up. The main reason for all that filtering is the level of investment in time and money that a separate business requires. Since those investment resources are limited, the decisions need to be meticulously weighed.

Portfolio

As of 2012 – 11 years after it was founded – CbusineZ had a portfolio with 16 ventures, two of which had not yet fully matured into a company. Development in that 11-year period followed an S curve, as shown in Figure 1.7.

After CbusineZ was established, a number of businesses were launched in short order. The pace slackened in the years that followed, but recently more ventures have been started. A few years ago CbusineZ redoubled its efforts to achieve growth by hiring more people. De Groot expected to have several new ventures in the portfolio again by the end of 2012. 'Actually, we are also seeing ventures merge together. We set up almost every venture separately and now we're seeing businesses grow together. We've concluded that a merger makes those companies stronger. By the end of the year, we'll probably be back to 16 ventures in total', he said at the time.

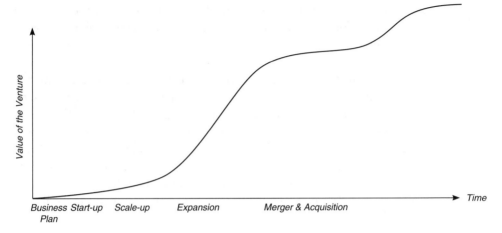

Figure 1.7 Venture development over time

CbusineZ introduced its portfolio approach in 2011, under which it defined four core themes for ventures: (1) enabling self-management, (2) quality improvement, (3) cost reduction and (4) availability of care (see Box 1.1). There is actually also a fifth theme, that of providing general and technical support through a consultancy or web design firm, for instance. These small ancillary businesses make it easier and cheaper to establish new ventures.

BOX 1.1

Enabling self-management

- Creating infrastructure and processes for self-management

Quality improvement

- Develop and disseminate best practices for quality assurance
- Benchmarking
- Provide advice and IT support for health care processes

Cost reduction

- Introduce efficient processes
- Share infrastructure with other parties

Availability of care

- Champion unique, innovative options that fail to materialize or are in danger of failing
- Provide solutions for bottlenecks to large-scale provision of health care options
- Promote health care options with proprietary rights of strategic interest to CZ

'We examine which themes are thriving and which are stagnating in terms of the overall portfolio', De Groot says. 'Then we can explicitly redirect our activities accordingly. At the same time, though, we're business-minded enough to realize that the balance tends to swing toward the theme with the most potential'.

Staffing the team

To a large degree the staffing of a venture will determine its success. An organization needs various types of people at various stages in the venturing process who are capable of completing that particular part of the process. De Groot's team consists of entrepreneurial people. 'The seven business managers are all builders and go-getters. They can provide a venture with excellent guidance through the start-up and expansion stages, but someone is needed who can see it through for the long term', De Groot explains. The type of venture is, of course, also an important factor in choosing a business manager to do the work.

The composition of the current team of business managers at CbusineZ stems from relying on long-time staff members on one side, and a targeted recruitment policy on the other. That policy is based on looking at two things: (1) what component someone is knowledgeable about and (2) the skills someone possesses. CbusineZ specifically determines for each business manager the venture to which they are best suited.

Some business managers are in charge of more than one venture, unless, of course, their venture is so large that it requires their full-time attention. Rotating between ventures keeps the business managers on their toes and helps disseminate experience among the various ventures. CbusineZ recently adopted a philosophy whereby a business manager returns to the central venturing organization periodically to get back to the primary business of idea evaluation and business plan development. De Groot says:

> We are alert to the right triggers here and you can lose sight of those triggers when you are always doing business. Here, we train people more, so their analytical powers grow. I prefer to keep them back here for a while before sending them back out, but it doesn't always work out that way. Sometimes a business manager has only just returned to our home base when an opportunity arises. Well, then he's back out there in no time. That's also part of entrepreneurship. When an opportunity arises, we jump on it. It's all part of the game.

Coordination between CbusineZ and CZ

CbusineZ is housed at CZ headquarters. In fact, in recent years the venturing organization has relied even more heavily on the knowledge and expertise of the CZ staff. For instance, they have turned more frequently to their colleagues at CZ at the start of a project, so that together they can assess the strategic value for the parent organization of a potential venture. One added benefit of this is that it immediately instils enthusiasm for the products or services of a potential venture among future users or purchasers.

It is important to consciously create some distance between the venturing organization and the parent organization, while at the same time deliberately building in some connections. Given that the culture at insurance companies is not exactly innovative, that distance they create is necessary to allow them the freedom to be entrepreneurial. On the other hand, it is important not to stray too far from the parent organization because then you run the risk of the parent organization not knowing about or using the products and services developed. 'It is vital to have a linking pin who can keep the parent organization apprised of what we're doing', De Groot points out. 'That person will tell colleagues about what we have to offer. Many venturing organizations underestimate the importance of this. For that matter, even the literature on corporate venturing underestimates the usefulness and necessity of alliance with the parent organization'.

And this is what makes setting up ventures so difficult. The venturing organization can offer or promote a new product or service to the parent organization, but they are not obliged to buy it. Fortunately, since CbusineZ is positioned as an independent entity at the Board of Directors level, the management at the parent organization has a tendency to jump at the partnership opportunities presented. In the case of Psy Health Direct, the parent organization also provided a form of turnover guarantee. As part of that formal agreement, CZ pays a penalty if purchases fall below a certain point.

While CbusineZ has been steadily professionalizing, De Groot still has one more thing he would like to see happen to improve the coordination process. 'The degree to which you can formally arrange matters with the parent organization is always uncertain', he says. 'Value ultimately lies in the way the parent organization interfaces with the venture and that could certainly be managed more stringently'. De Groot is referring to things such as the creation of participation agreements, corporate governance rules and articles of association. The aims and objectives would then be immediately clear to everyone.

The organizational units for support services, such as IT, Finance and HRM, are well partitioned from the parent organization. These services are very tightly managed from the central office, something that might not work as well for a venturing organization such as CbusineZ. When it comes to ventures, one has to be flexible, be able to change gear quickly and have focus. Central services at the parent company are not always very comfortable with this. That is why services like those mentioned above are organized as distinct entities within the venturing organization.

The independence of the venturing organization cannot be captured in a ready-made structure through an alliance with the parent organization. There is no model that concretely lays out how to do that. It is an ongoing question of customization and human interaction.

Advancing insights

Each year, CbusineZ uses stage gates to re-examine developments in the market. 'Every year we run our ventures through the CVM paces to see how they're growing', De Groot explains:

> We've developed all kinds of names in the process. Poorly operating initiatives are labelled a 'flatliner' or 'zombie' [Figure 1.8]. Cases like that cause us to ask ourselves what the problem could be. If it's just an internal issue, we can examine whether it's worth investing some more to pull the venture out of the fire. But as soon as it becomes apparent that there's no market for the product, it's better to end things.

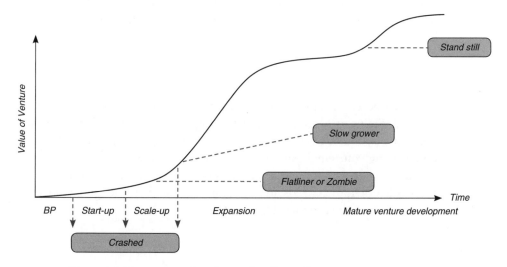

Figure 1.8 Venture type identification by CbusineZ

As a rule, CbusineZ can resolve these issues at the preliminary stage. If the process is already further underway it attempts to re-launch the venture by taking measures such as replacing the management.

Psy Health Direct is now on the verge of migrating from the start-up to the expansion stage, where the challenge is to cash in on the growth and claim market share. As part of that CbusineZ is trying to form a coalition with a number of innovation-minded mental health care institutions in the Netherlands of reasonable size. The coalition is united by a belief in the benefits of internet use as a tool in the health care sector. In addition, the product is available to other insurers. If it were up to CbusineZ, these parties would be able to purchase a licence or even participate in the joint venture. 'Our ultimate goal is to manage CZ's strategic value. If another insurer joins the ranks, that adds volume. That contributes to the strategic objectives', says De Groot.

One recent and considerable threat has been an overly optimistic estimate of the pace of change in the business market. In the life-cycle model this pertains to Stage 2, which involves the expansion stage that follows the start-up stage. Sales lead times proved longer than anticipated. The forecasts for Psy Health Direct were based on indicators from previous ventures, but the criteria for it were apparently different. Although the contact with the business market went smoothly, the registration of employees with mental health issues has been sluggish. 'The frustrating thing is that you have to make an estimate up front based on certain assumptions. But that estimate only gets borne out, or not, in practice', says De Groot. The consequence of slower market adoption for a product is that one needs more working capital than originally calculated. Expectations are that it will take a year longer than anticipated before the patient registration increases. More large-scale clients are joining the initiative though, which is a sign of the underlying potential.

In market-based ventures, sales are generally the trickiest part, because they involve building up something from nothing – not just the product or service, but also a customer base. And one has to learn what really works: 'You end up changing your emphasis along the way. We've noticed that clients have questions when we tell them about the product. When they proceed to tell us about what their own needs are, sometimes you end up changing your story or even parts of the product', De Groot points out.

Everybody wins

The eventual profit model will be based not so much on generating turnover at Psy Health Direct, although that is naturally important to CbusineZ. The real benefit will lie with the insurers that use this product, such as CZ. By purchasing this product, insurers in the business market can save over €2000 per patient being treated. This method could even result in a parent organization deciding to keep a non-profitable venture running, since it could save the Purchasing department of the parent organization enough to compensate for the venture's losses.

It is interesting to note the lack of fierce competition among insurers when it comes to these kinds of ventures, though De Groot points out that this depends heavily on the type of venture involved: an initiative that could help an insurer gain a better market position will be protected against competitors. But for innovations aimed at customers, there are many more opportunities for cooperation. After all, they are basically social corporations whose objective is to keep health care as available as possible. 'You obviously still want to win in the commercial sphere', De Groot says. 'But you also know very well that there is no point in competing with one another over e-health and internet products. That's where you should join together'.

2

Corporate venturing in the chemical industry: a colourful case*

Jessica van den Bosch and Stijn van den Hoogen

AkzoNobel first started its venturing endeavours in 2002, with the establishment of 'AkzoNobel New Ventures'. Just eight years later though, that initiative was ended. Now (2013) it is on the verge of launching a new venture organization. What can venturing do for AkzoNobel? What can the new venture organization learn from the old 'New Ventures'? And what mistakes must they avoid?

The seed of an idea

His business card lists him as the 'Director of Technology & Open Innovation' – words that have coloured Jos Keurentjes' daily work life since

2012. What they amount to is designing the long-term technology strategy for AkzoNobel. Before Keurentjes held this position, he was the technology director of one of the company's business units for five years.

In early 2012, Keurentjes sat down at the table with Graeme Armstrong, the member of AkzoNobel's Executive Committee responsible for Research, Development and Innovation (RD&I). Armstrong wanted to create a long-term innovation strategy but did not yet have a solid idea for how to do it. 'His basic notion was clearly aimed at having a bit of technological content, along with extracting a bit of entrepreneurship', Keurentjes recalls.

AkzoNobel

AkzoNobel is one of the world's largest paints and coatings companies and a major producer of speciality chemicals. Its paints are sold for both consumer and professional markets. AkzoNobel performance coatings are used in an array of industrial paint applications, encompassing a host of technological features, such as coatings for ships and coil coatings, coating systems for steel frames, powder coatings and car repair systems. Products from its chemicals division are sold almost exclusively through business-to-business outlets. The chemicals it manufactures run the entire gamut from large bulk products on the one hand, to fairly small-scale, specific applications on the other. Among the company's better-known paint brands are big names like Sikkens and Dulux.

The company originated in the Netherlands but has acquired Anglo-Saxon influences in the wake of several takeovers, which have also introduced changes into the company culture. AkzoNobel is headquartered in Amsterdam, with operations in 80 countries and some 50 000 employees. In 2012, it managed to solidify its position as a global leader in sustainability by assuming the top ranking in the Chemistry super sector of the prestigious Dow Jones Sustainability World Indices (DJSI). AkzoNobel had been included among that index's top three since 2007.

In the mid-1990s, AkzoNobel was organized into business units, each with its own profit-and-loss accountability. As a result of this restructuring, many divisions in the company have become compartmentalized over the past ten to 15 years. Keurentjes explains:

> Sometimes a business unit might have a variety of sub-business units. This led to a strongly market-driven culture, highly focused on one's own particular business and today's markets. Among the business units there were, of course, a few that

might have pursued a connection with an outside party, but this was almost always in the context of outsourcing some of the work.

AkzoNobel New Ventures

In the 1990s the company had a large R&D department in Arnhem, where over 1000 employees conducted research for various business units, though the chemical engineering arm accounted for the greatest share of that. In the decade that followed, activities there were sharply curtailed. This is not to say that everyone who worked there was fired. Many of them were transferred to the business units they had been doing research for, producing a situation in which the focus of activities shifted much more from the long term to the short term, since each business unit's primary concern was, of course, its immediate customers. This prompted the management at AkzoNobel to set up a separate unit. The shift from corporate R&D to research that was integrated primarily into business unit activities had made the company vulnerable to the risk of missing out on new developments. Under that construction, the business units were primarily focused on the upcoming quarter, their budgets and serving their existing clients.

This led to the formation, in 2002, of AkzoNobel New Ventures. That organizational unit was a separate business for developing (or further developing) innovations, with a substantial budget for investing in new ventures that grew out of AkzoNobel Chemicals and included the involvement of outside parties, so-called collaborative venturing. AkzoNobel New Ventures fell directly under the Board of Management (Chemicals) and was supervised by a venture panel made up of a delegation of senior managers from Chemicals' business units. The panel met five to six times a year to examine the portfolio and assess its progress. They were the ones who decided whether a venture could proceed to the next stage. Mike Zeitler was in charge of the day-to-day operations involved in setting up the new business unit from the start. AkzoNobel New Ventures launched over 15 ventures from its inception in 2002 to when it was dissolved in 2010: six or seven of these were very successful.

In 2008, Harmen Kielstra, as ventures manager, was responsible for the New Ventures portfolio. He made sure that the individual ventures were making enough progress, all reporting was done on time and any issues were identified as early as possible. He also prepared new ventures for the venture panel. Kielstra says:

> The energy was like nothing I'd experienced before, because you were dealing with ventures that were truly at the embryonic stage. They literally involved someone

who had invented a molecule that didn't have a use within his or her own business unit but did have prospects for other markets.

The venturing process at AkzoNobel New Ventures was organized in distinct stages, the so-called stage gates (see Figure P.1 in the Preface). The first stage was the idea-generating stage. Many ideas presented to the New Ventures team did indeed concern such new discoveries, but they also addressed issues a business unit had been struggling with, which had been 'floating around' for too long, or ones with an above-average risk profile. People would then approach New Ventures and ask them how they would handle it. 'But the unique thing about what we were doing was that it was always fundamentally market-oriented', Kielstra points out.

Because so many ideas were coming in from so many different areas, the process for categorizing those ideas could sometimes be a little unstructured. And the focus on which ideas should be developed for securing the future of AkzoNobel was often missing. This lack of focus was partly caused by the fact that they had a reasonably well-filled portfolio of ventures, which had to be managed by a relatively small team of four staff members.

Once an idea started to become more concrete, it entered the second stage: drafting the Venture Brief, as it was called. Over the course of three to six months, a preliminary business case would be built. This was the period for considering questions such as: what kind of market is there? How many potential customers are there? What are the exact margins in that business? How should this be approached? Can we do it on our own or do we need to bring in another party? What will our role in the entire supply chain be? Kielstra recalls:

> That means you have to jump in, feel things out and write it all up fairly quickly. We would bring people in to help us and they enjoyed it – people who held a technological position but were ready for a new challenge and needed to expand their horizons; our own personnel, who would then be freed up to work part-time on this for three, or five to six, months. So, that also had an incredibly strong HR development effect. We hadn't done it for that purpose, but if you asked all the people who were involved what they thought about the experience, they would say that was the cherry on top.

Stage three was that of writing the Venture Plan. This covered the same themes as the Venture Brief, but everything was worked out into a proper business plan with much more detail than in a Venture Brief. This was also the stage at which discussions were held with outsiders and alliances formed.

The Venture Plan was generally written by the same person who drew up the Venture Brief, although that did not always prove such a good choice. 'You need a very specific kind of expertise to roll out a product or technology', says Kielstra. 'Moreover, the underlying thinking was that the owner of the Venture Plan would also be responsible for organizing the subsequent stages of the pilot process and the market launch, but that's not something everybody can do'.

As soon as the panel had decided to approve the Venture Plan, the pilot stage was initiated. 'Actually, the pilot stage was more of a lead-up stage to the launch', Kielstra clarifies. 'There was still one kind of check after the pilot, but there was basically no more turning back, since, in most cases, the level of investment was too high'. After the pilot stage, therefore, the venture would pretty much automatically proceed to the launch.

Business unit Pulp & Paper: a new venture

One of the ventures Kielstra experienced first-hand was that of Pulp & Paper Chemicals. This business unit at AkzoNobel is involved in the worldwide production of the chemicals used in the production processes for making paper. The unit's added value goes well beyond merely supplying chemicals for turning intermediate goods into finished products to include the knowledge and expertise from AkzoNobel about the chemicals' properties (advisory services).

In 2005, a colleague from Sweden discovered a new application. 'A business development manager figured out how we could capture NOx [nitrogen oxide] and mercury from power plant exhaust through a very effective process. So, we had discovered a process that was built on our existing products', Kielstra explains. This offered a very attractive new prospect that could be used to generate additional revenue in the energy business.

A venture manager started working on the Venture Brief based on the initial test results. It all looked very promising. And even though the new application would require only a relatively modest investment for each coal-fired power plant, the volume of potential orders was substantial enough to make the return on investment very interesting. 'It was really such a gorgeous no-brainer that you just knew: this is going to take off. Eventually, every coal-fired plant in America will have to have this. Every new coal-fired plant in China will have to have this. And we're going to do it', Kielstra recalls.

The venture panel was equally enthusiastic and the venture team was given the go-ahead to write the Venture Plan. The deeper investigation required at this stage revealed a number of challenges, however. While the costs still appeared manageable, modifying a process at a coal-fired plant that runs 24/7 is no picnic. 'As so often happens: fantastic idea, then you zoom in and end up on a rollercoaster ride that leaves you thinking, "But this is impossible", which is only logical. How could we paper guys even begin to think we could do such a thing?' says Kielstra.

Outside entrepreneurs with specific industry knowledge were brought in to help write the Venture Plan. What's more, they were prepared to invest in the project, too. That would cut into AkzoNobel's margins, but according to Kielstra this was also often the fastest way to get to the pilot and launch. Not to mention that it would add credibility in the eyes of the venture panel if an outside party besides AkzoNobel New Ventures recognized the added value of the idea and was prepared to invest in the venture, as well. At the same time, it would secure the parent company's support for the venture, since once they entered into a partnership with outsiders, people would not be so eager to pull the plug. So, it was also a way to advance the venture process.

In 2008, three years after the venture manager had started writing the Venture Brief, the project was ready to enter the pilot stage. Kielstra says:

> There was a lot of trial and error but eventually we thought we arrived at where we needed to be. There were a few issues that still needed attention, such as wastewater that was a few degrees too hot. Relatively easy to fix on the face of it – just cool it down, but that requires adding energy. And if we didn't have to do that, we could sell it as a CO_2-neutral process. The intellectual property rights also presented a considerable challenge, because the process was actually simple and had been done before.

In 2009, the Pulp & Paper venture was ended without ever getting to the pilot stage. What had happened?

Practical lessons

Normally, the step from plan to action is made at the pilot stage. That turned out to be particularly problematic in this case, because AkzoNobel New Ventures could not provide the parent company 100 per cent certainty with regard to the functionality from a technological standpoint. Whereas Kielstra's team was convinced that it would work, with the right people, the parent company insisted on having concrete proof that it worked before it was prepared to approve the investments.

There was also an unfortunate confluence of circumstances. A shift in personnel among some senior roles at the Pulp & Paper business unit created a situation in which the venture lost its top-of-mind status for the business unit's management. Kielstra points out:

> Meanwhile, we were walking around with dollar signs in our eyes and thinking, 'Yeah, guys, we're going to start something new and AkzoNobel is going to get a new business unit, all from existing technology. Fantastic!' It was hard to believe. Here you are, you can do something to help the environment, something that uses AkzoNobel's existing technology and requires little change to the infrastructure of new customers, and we still couldn't make it happen.

This case shows just how important timing is. Kielstra admits:

> Maybe Mike and I should have seen it coming, should've asked ourselves what the stakeholders in the company were all about. If we had pushed a bit harder, been a bit more daring, Mike and I probably could've saved it, and then this could've been the new billion AkzoNobel was looking for. But that is all with hindsight, of course.

As important as timing is, this case also demonstrates that the way venturing is structured within the parent company is critical for success. In the end the connection to the parent company through the involvement of the Board of Management and the various business units (in the form of the venture panel) provided no guarantee for bringing the venture to life. The catch-22 created by the technological functionality issue and the associated investment caused the process to stall. Senior changes at the top were a second obstacle that interfered with the pilot launch. If, to top it all off, the arena in which you operate as an organization undergoes drastic change (global crisis), it is going to be a major challenge to continue with long-term and/or high-risk innovation projects in many large corporations.

The end of AkzoNobel New Ventures

The global crisis of 2008 finally prompted the parent company to end its corporate venturing activities in 2010 and thus close down AkzoNobel New Ventures. Kielstra explains:

> The leadership at the time was not a fan of the model, because it was only being used in the speciality chemicals business area and had not produced enough revenue after seven years. Also, the prevailing opinion at the time was that a business unit should be able to manage its long-term affairs on its own. Whether

that involved developments in the supply chain or in technology, it was the business unit's responsibility and the task of the Board of Management to promote that.

It is essential for venture organizations to have staying power: developing and launching ventures costs a great deal of time and financial investment. The turnaround time for technological ventures can easily run into eight to ten years. 'By that point, we had been investing millions every year for seven, eight years', says Kielstra. 'You know those hockey stick charts, where you project revenues over the course of time [Figure 2.1]? We simply hadn't produced that yet, and after a while business people lose patience'.

The dismantling of AkzoNobel New Ventures in 2010 caused two ventures that were still underway to be stopped. AkzoNobel still owns the intellectual property rights for those ventures, so perhaps there is a chance that it could derive some benefit from them in the future. The remaining ventures were either incorporated into existing business units at the parent company or sold to other companies, with the new owners acquiring the staff and/or intellectual property rights. Kielstra says:

> When we were told to clean out the entire venture portfolio, everyone who was actively involved in the individual ventures landed on their feet. Those who remained at the company managed to get a promotion out of it; a couple of people who sought work elsewhere even ended up with dream jobs.

In hindsight, he realizes that they had always done that part well: they had always had the right people working for them in the ventures.

A new beginning

So, here we are several years later, and the need to actively structure innovation is still alive at AkzoNobel. The old venturing model and thinking behind AkzoNobel New Ventures revolved primarily around developing new opportunities outside the business units, which, if proven successful, would then be brought back into the business units. There was no clear vision for the future incorporated into the portfolio that could serve as a basis for new ventures.

That is why the present efforts aim to identify the technology platforms out there that AkzoNobel might want to use in the future. The knowledge and experience contained in those platforms needs to be integrated into the organization in due course, and Keurentjes is convinced that venturing is an important instrument for achieving that. The strategic motivation

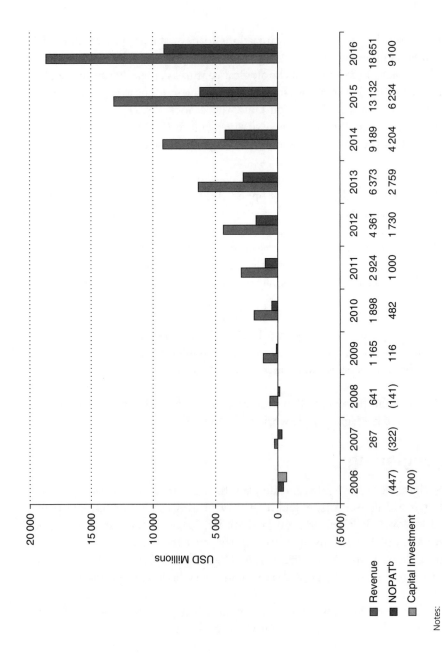

	2006	2007	2008	2009	2010	2011	2012	2013	2014	2015	2016
Revenue		267	641	1 165	1 898	2 924	4 361	6 373	9 189	13 132	18 651
NOPAT[b]		(322)	(141)	116	482	1 000	1 730	2 759	4 204	6 234	9 100
Capital Investment	(447)	(700)									

Notes:

a. A hockey stick projection is one that shows its last few years of actual results as flat, and then rockets up for future years like the blade of a hockey stick.

b. Net Operating Profit After Tax.

Figure 2.1 Hockey stick projection[a] of revenue over time

for corporate venturing, therefore, lies primarily in creating a competitive product portfolio for the future.

Add to that the fact that the window of opportunity for R&D in terms of developing new products is an average of two years. The turnaround time for the academic research programmes AkzoNobel participates in is actually relatively long. It can take just two years before the research even starts, which then runs for four to five years, at which point it still needs to be actually converted into something tangible. 'You're talking about time horizons that can easily exceed ten years', Keurentjes points out. 'As you can see, there's a huge gap between the two years of our current focus and the ten years that takes'. And that is exactly what he plans to focus on: filling that gap through venturing activities. Keurentjes says:

> Venturing allows you to flesh out a few relatively short-term endeavours that fit in the portfolio. Of course, it does mean that you have to piggyback onto groups that are doing a kind of next-generation thing – projects that aren't necessarily early stage, but just past that, which must typically prove themselves as a viable business within five years.

Form plus content

Keurentjes is currently working on a new model for pursuing corporate venturing within AkzoNobel. He says:

> To establish the venturing on a somewhat solid footing and do something for all of the designated technology platforms, you're easily talking about 100 million if you would follow the approach most companies do. This option is currently difficult to realize, so we are now thinking about another possible strategy.

The idea for the new model is simple and two-pronged. To start with, AkzoNobel will look for partnerships with start-ups that are currently developing a technology that could eventually benefit AkzoNobel, which would thus fit into the defined strategic portfolio. At the same time, it will search for venture capitalists (VCs) who might be interested in financing that start-up. By participating as the launching customer itself, AkzoNobel hopes that the VCs will be more willing to come through with the funding. 'We still have to fully flesh out that idea and come up with the exact procedures. Is this something you can formalize or would it have to be an ad hoc system? I don't have the answer yet, but it's easy to imagine that it could work', says Keurentjes.

This raises the question of whether AkzoNobel should, for instance, also acquire shares in the start-ups. Following on from that is the issue of how to ensure that the new technology does indeed wind up in the hands of the large organization. This is a vital issue for many companies when it comes to corporate venturing: the connection to the parent company.

Another dilemma concerns whether or not other parties, in addition to AkzoNobel, can be launching customers. Keurentjes recalls:

> Last week, I uttered the words 'co-competitor development' for the first time, and then really stirred up the pot by linking them to 'PPG'. That is the major competitor for everyone in the coatings business, both deco and performance coatings. What I actually said was, 'We should pursue some developments together with PPG'. People looked at me in complete astonishment, but I might give it a try.

In the past at AkzoNobel New Ventures, spin-ins – whereby a new venture was kept within the existing business unit – did not always work so well. The main reason for that, according to Keurentjes, is that start-ups with revenue of less than ten million get swallowed up in a business unit the size of a typical Akzo company (with an average volume of one billion). Keurentjes continues:

> They don't get sufficient attention from the business, because they are too small, and a venture like that will suffocate to death in no time under all the rules there are. Then it can't get off the ground. So, you have to figure out a way for it to mature in such a manner that it can actually generate, say, something like 100 million in revenue.

But how can you help it reach that level within AkzoNobel? Keurentjes is focusing his efforts on creating a separate business unit with a strong focus on the portfolio of ventures under development, with the added ambition of being budget-neutral from the very beginning. As soon as the ventures are mature (generating sufficient revenue), you can examine whether they are ready to either be incorporated into existing business units (spin-ins) or continue on their own as independent organizations (spin-outs).

Four operational elements in the venture process

How are venturing endeavours to be organized within a new ventures company? And will a model be used to streamline the process? Does AkzoNobel have a clear vision for the future as a foundation for defining a portfolio that will govern the choice of ventures to be developed? And, how will people be brought in to the ventures? What will their relationship to the venture organization and/or parent company be? The final element touches on the connection a new venture will have with the parent company: how will this be arranged? Is it based on deliberate policy or advancing insights? Each of these elements will be discussed below, both in terms of how they were handled at Kielstra's AkzoNobel New Ventures and how Keurentjes sees them playing out in the new venture organization.

Use of a model

It is fairly common practice in the world of corporate venturing to use a stage-gate process. Such step-by-step models help organizations monitor whether various pre-established conditions are being met. This knowledge can then be used to decide whether to continue on to the next phase or kill the project.

AkzoNobel New Ventures

AkzoNobel New Ventures relied on a stage-gate model. Using the five stages shown in Figure P.1 in the Preface as a basis, the venture panel would decide whether or not to promote a venture to the next stage. But the New Ventures team could also exert some influence by thoroughly preparing for the meetings and having all the necessary information ready in time. Kielstra admits:

> Looking back critically at our performance, I would say that we didn't necessarily adhere to the stage-gate model too strictly, that we didn't define the milestones too definitively, but were instead more committed, through our enthusiasm and belief in the inherent potential, to having each venture succeed and taking it to the next stage. The documents were finished on time, everybody was professional, but from the stage-gate standpoint, I'd have to say we did not do enough analyses at the portfolio level.

The literature refers to this tendency of policy-makers to stick to certain procedures despite the fact that they are not producing successful results as 'escalation of commitment'.

The new venture organization

'As a rule, we are very good at starting projects but very bad at bringing them to fruition', says Keurentjes:

> I think that's fairly common: it's something every company struggles with. You are always tempted to keep slugging away at it, and those research fellows can always come up with some reason for sticking it out. But at some point, you have to also

be able to say: we're pulling the plug. It's not going to work or it won't yield what we thought it would.

Some companies are more flexible in applying the stage-gate model in their organization than others. Based on Kielstra's experiences, it seems desirable in the new venture organization to institute more clear-cut points at which the decision could be made to end a venture. On the other hand, you could argue that in the beginning start-ups do not have any fixed focus and tend to meander: that is actually their strength.

There is a tendency in many stage-gate processes to set a predetermined outcome at the mouth of the development funnel (see Preface), then try to get to it in more or less a straight line. Keurentjes' vision is that the outcome is what could vary over time and that you then reposition the funnel to reach a different goal. As he points out:

> If you were to only shoot directly at that first outcome, then you would throw it out at the second stage gate. You would have to say, 'This isn't going to deliver the outcome'. But the question is: could it deliver another outcome and where would you then start in your new funnel? You wouldn't have to start all the way back at the beginning but could insert a new funnel, maybe vertically and maybe just slightly back in the process.

Keurentjes still advocates for a flexible stage-gate process. 'Instinctively, I am not convinced at the outset that a highly rigid and strict stage-gate process is the way to go. I'm sure you do need it, but what the best way of employing it is . . . I haven't entirely figured that out', he says. There is no suitable alternative model for the stage-gate process. The tricky part is that you want to maintain flexibility in terms of implementing ventures, without compromising your ability to create potential stopping points. Moreover, that dilemma is different for each organization and venture and cannot be easily defined in terms of specific guidelines.

Portfolio

Organizations use portfolios to signify strategic fields in which they would like to work toward a given status in certain areas. Portfolios provide a framework for assessing new activities in terms of whether or not they fit in with that strategic picture. Beyond that though, they also provide an instant overview of the distribution of activities: are these fairly evenly spread out or is all of the attention and money going solely toward one part of the specified field?

AkzoNobel New Ventures

The underlying premise for AkzoNobel New Ventures, from the very beginning, was always that more thought had to be put into the long term, but there was no clear portfolio perspective defined ahead of time. 'The venture activities were driven more by the fact that there were some trends in the market that the business units were in danger of missing out on', says Kielstra. 'There was no well-executed, thorough analysis at the portfolio level; what they were trying to address, primarily, was the focus of individual ventures and the overall market needs. In the meantime, AkzoNobel, as parent company, did undergo a few big portfolio changes through divestments and acquisitions'.

The new venture organization

Keurentjes has already identified a number of themes for AkzoNobel where there is a need for development within certain technology platforms and these collectively determine the strategic focus.

The first example is in process technology. These are the processes used to make things, which result in new production technologies. As Keurentjes says:

> So, for example, we want to be able to ensure that researchers can make the right molecules, give them the right structure: balls, particles, bubbles, whatever. It is particularly important for paint systems that you be able to play around with those factors and right now we don't have much of a take on it.

Another trend at -AkzoNobel is the desire to not build large plants anymore and instead concentrate on small units, located near the customers. This introduces greater flexibility and the capital investments are lower.

The second example involves smart materials. The two most important functions for a coating are protection and decoration, for instance through colour. Right now there is a profusion of developments in the area of materials that add an additional function to those. Examples include coatings that repel insects (possibly very useful for fighting malaria) and coatings capable of temporarily storing energy.

That second application falls under the broader theme of 'energy technology'. Many developments in the market today are paving the way towards an energy supply that is largely regulated per household. Interest in solar panels is growing exponentially, for instance, the problem with that application in countries such as the Netherlands being that the sun only shines between noon and three in the afternoon. And that is not generally the time of day you need the energy being generated; it is primarily in the evenings that you need that electricity. Keurentjes points out:

> In Germany they're already running intelligent systems that give households the option of either pulling power off the grid or supplying it to the grid. They have, however, had a few instances when the entire system tripped around mid-day, because there was too much power being sent to the grid in a manner that the grid had not been designed to handle. That means that we probably have to move toward systems that can buffer the energy for a single household or a small cluster of buildings. Storage in some form or other, such as with smart coatings or small-scale conversion technology, could be one solution.

The answer could lie then with something like capacitive coatings, which could be used to store the energy for a few hours a day. If interior house paint, for instance, could do that, then it would acquire valuable added functionality, besides just adding colour to your walls. 'These are trends that we are highly aware of, but where our own knowledge is sadly lacking: we simply don't possess it. So, that is clearly a part of the game where the venturing piece is really going to play an important role', Keurentjes adds.

A third suggested theme lies in the area of industrial biotechnology. As Keurentjes points out:

> A large part of reducing our carbon footprint will involve using raw materials from renewable resources. We would be sourcing those largely from suppliers. In addition, the technology needed to do this [bio-refinery] could be a new market for us to deliver chemicals, technology and services to. We still have to develop the exact business model, but this would be a very productive way to help close the life cycle loop in the value chains we operate in.

In total, AkzoNobel thinks it can define about ten platforms within these themes that it expects to be essential to its business operations within ten years' time. These platforms are being addressed from two vantage points: on the one hand, they are used as a framework for academic development programmes, such as Horizon 2020; on the other, planners envision establishing a definite venturing strategy for each one.

Venture team composition

Organizations have different methods for putting together their venture teams. In some cases, for instance, they assemble a team that is responsible for organizing all of a company's ventures (venture managers). They then put them in touch with a content director for each particular venture to oversee the technological content.

AkzoNobel New Ventures

The management of AkzoNobel New Ventures comprised four staff members: a general manager, a controller, a ventures' manager and an assistant. The composition of the venture teams, which is to say the people providing daily leadership of each new venture being established, was always venture-driven. Kielstra says:

> Each time we wanted to start a new venture, we asked ourselves the question of who could do it and what business it would fit in with. Because of my role as portfolio manager, I naturally spent a lot of time visiting all the parts of our organization, which made me highly visible. So, people were always coming up to me on their own.

Kielstra did not have a fixed profile that the venture managers had to meet, no list of competencies. Due to the very nature of the activities, a venture attracts people who are not afraid of a slightly higher risk profile. 'We always had a list of people who had expressed an interest in participating', says Kielstra. 'And we were also often good at finding the people who had something to contribute, for the simple reason that there are not that many people who understand both the technology and the product–market combination'.

The fact that a venture operates outside the normal organization is also conducive. Kielstra recalls:

> Many of the things you have to do as part of the venturing process require that you sometimes circumvent corporate rules. And in a standard business, you simply cannot do that. If everyone were to do that, it would be a mess. And this was part of that. We didn't need HR: Mike and I were there, just like entrepreneurs, and we would say, 'Okay, here's our goal: who's going to make it happen? What do you think?' Then we'd discuss it for an hour and decide who we wanted to call.

The new venture organization

Keurentjes is now in the process of assembling the team that will pursue the venturing efforts at AkzoNobel:

I started as a small independent operator, but it became rapidly clear that all this requires a significant team. On one hand we have the technical experts who evaluate the opportunities for their technical and commercial merits. They closely connect with the experts from Finance to see how we can best tackle the financial side of a given opportunity. For the academic developments, we see a major role for the European Horizon 2020 programme, to allow the execution of projects that will become important for us on a longer term. We now have quite a team present in Brussels to identify and drive the opportunities.

Equally important is the work currently being done on the details in terms of defining the themes and associated platforms, in addition to designing the venturing unit. These three interests all run parallel and require the necessary landscaping. Keurentjes explains: 'Which academic groups are the ones that know about what matters in this field? Where can we find all those small companies that are going to do great things? That is the landscape where we'll find the parties we want to work with'.

At the moment, it is far from clear how all this will be organized. Since any endeavour will probably involve a combined interest between a VC and AkzoNobel, it will have to be tackled in a smart manner. 'I can imagine that we will have to give these ventures a great deal of freedom', Keurentjes surmises, 'so that we don't quash their entrepreneurial spirit under the rules and procedures of a large organization. But at the same time, they'll have to be tightly managed. I expect, then, that it will be primarily an operation at arm's length'.

Connection to the parent company

The reasons for investing in corporate venturing are always fundamentally strategic. It is a way for a company to achieve innovations that will have added value for its organization. It is therefore essential to not only think about how that added value is going to be provided, but also ensure that it is well received.

AkzoNobel New Ventures

The fundamental premise behind AkzoNobel New Ventures was that the technologies or applications under development had to eventually complement the activities of one of the existing business units. That means the venture process was always aimed at integrating the innovations (spin-ins). The reason for accomplishing this through AkzoNobel New Ventures was mostly due to the difficulty or expense of achieving certain kinds of innovations within the business units themselves. But there was also the advantage that an application could then be made available to other business units and its value would go beyond that single business unit.

According to Kielstra, the most difficult part of the entire process was once the introduction had been successful and they already had their first customers and had generated some revenue. 'That was the point at which you had to approach a business and get the venture integrated into it', he says:

> In theory, the connection could be quickly explained in meetings, but the business units have rules and agendas dictated by the parent organization that they have to follow and that influence the timing of the integration. The end of the year, for example, can be a difficult time, because the budgets have just been drawn up and no financial provisions were made for an internal takeover of a venture with its associated assets.

Even though organizational integration had been well planned (unit fell directly under the Board of Management; involvement of business unit managers secured through the venture panel), the operational connection proved difficult. One aspect that had been very deliberately introduced by Zeitler and Kielstra with regard to creating a connection between ventures and business units was to enlist people from the business unit that the venture would probably later be incorporated into. So, as soon as it became clear where the venture would eventually end up, they would actively instil engagement by appointing someone from that business unit at the venture part-time.

'How did that work? Well, Mister X might work for the venture 60 per cent of the time and for the business unit the remaining 40 per cent', explains Kielstra:

> This was mostly from a desire on the part of Mister X to be able to return to the business unit if the venture did not result in a launch. Even though we managed to engage entrepreneurial people, the degree of uncertainty and the impact that has on someone's career always played a role – all the more so since we were bringing in senior-level people to the ventures who had already built an entire career at AkzoNobel and sometimes didn't want to put that at risk.

Despite, and perhaps because of, the level of involvement this created, it also posed some problems along the way – if, for example, the business unit's activities suddenly required extra attention just when the person was expected to give 200 per cent to the venture. 'The venture is much more fun', Kielstra points out, 'but also much more demanding, much less predictable. You might suddenly encounter a setback that you have to spend another five or six weeks trying to fix'.

Looking back at the operational elements listed above, how should the new venture unit be organized then? Should the stage-gate model be more stringently adhered to? Will a more clearly defined portfolio produce better results? What can be learned from the experiences with team composition for the purposes of the new unit? And what about the connection to the parent company: is it inevitably tricky?

The new venture organization

The model devised by Keurentjes for organizing venturing efforts within AkzoNobel does not yet have any best practices. The fact that the new venture unit plans to adopt the role of launching customer automatically links the start-up and parent company together. At the same time, though, this opens the door to the not-invented-here syndrome: the guys at corporate venturing can mess around a bit, but it does not tie in with the business. And 'we' in the business arm do all the work and earn all the money. 'That is one of those situations that's just part of the game, but that can actually be deadly for landing a venturing activity in the right spot', says Keurentjes.

For the time being, Keurentjes envisages that the start-ups will mostly benefit from the facilities the parent company can offer them to foster growth. These include not only organizational support (Legal, HR), but also operational support during the development process (use of laboratories, available know-how). 'It isn't until something truly starts to become a reality that you have to start thinking about how you're going to bring it home and whether it needs to be a spin-in or not', he adds.

Initial success

For the new venturing organization to succeed, it is important that it lands its initial success relatively quickly. 'One of the things I've already realized', says Keurentjes, 'is that we need to make sure that at least a couple of ventures are producing results by year three'. Those short-term results are also needed to give the ventures with longer turnaround times the time and space to fully develop. It is mostly important for the parent company to see those short-term results; then they will have confidence in the long-term results 'as a matter of course'.

NOTE

* In this case study, Jos Keurentjes expressed his personal views and opinions. He is therefore not necessarily speaking on behalf of AkzoNobel.

3

BAC BV: the successful exit of a Unilever spin-out

Jessica van den Bosch and Victor Gilsing

At the end of the nineteenth century, William Lever created Sunlight Soap with the goal of making hygiene universally available. In the early twentieth century, Lever's company joined together with several other manufacturers to form an industrial combination that would eventually result in a merger and form the seeds of the Unilever Company. The goals of promoting health and home and personal care, along with producing healthy foodstuffs, still form the core of the company's activities in 2014.

John Coombs joined Unilever as a management trainee in their engineer trainee programme. His career at Unilever grew – through engineering, factory management and consumer marketing – until in 2001 he learned that Unilever was talking about setting up a venture capital business. Coombs volunteered to design that business, together with a small team, and eventually became Managing Director of Unilever Ventures Europe.

Unilever Ventures

Unilever Ventures was established because Unilever was aiming to achieve organic growth in the developed world at that time. While the emerging markets enjoyed a very good level of organic growth, growth in developed markets was slower. In order to realize growth, Unilever considered venturing to be the most creative area of activity. 'In fact, we had worked with McKinsey to show that over the last 40 years, the best source of genuinely innovative new businesses was the combination of independent entrepreneurs working with venture capital', Coombs explains. Since that combina-

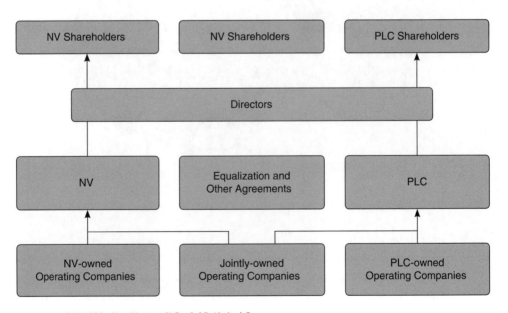

Note: NV = New Venture; PLC = Public Limited Company.

Figure 3.1 Unilever organogram

tion had proven successful, the idea was to implement it under the Unilever corporate umbrella (Figure 3.1).

BAC BV: a Unilever Ventures spin-out

Unilever Ventures is a management company that advises Unilever on its investments. It not only invests in start-ups, but also aims to spin out Unilever businesses that no longer form part of the parent company's core business. The most recent successful spin-out orchestrated by Unilever Ventures was BAC BV, which is being managed by Laurens Sierkstra.

After pursuing a degree in biology in Leiden and his doctoral research in biotechnology, Sierkstra landed a job with the laundry detergents division of Unilever in 1994. In 1997 Sierkstra was made Director of BAC BV, a wholly-owned subsidiary of Unilever that emerged out of the biotechnology research the company was performing through the 1980s and 1990s, primarily.

BAC BV manufactures products that are able to purify drugs in a highly targeted manner. Drugs produced through biological processes (biologics) have many impurities in them, as opposed to chemically synthesized drugs. Consider the case of vaccine manufacture, which relies primarily on eggs or other such biological systems. These systems contain certain impurities that get released in the process. Sierkstra explains:

> When it comes to research applications, we can produce the end products, which we supply to customers around the world. For products that are going to be used on a truly large scale, we partner with other companies. One of our main partners, for example, is GE Healthcare in Uppsala, Sweden.

In the late 1990s, Unilever decided to pursue the sale of several of its subsidiaries, mostly former speciality chemicals businesses. The purpose of the sale was primarily strategic; the company wanted to focus more strictly on its core business in laundry detergents and food products. At the time, BAC BV was working on a project that was important to Unilever, so it was not included in the divestitures, but the parent company's interest in biotechnology waned significantly and the sources of income declined. BAC BV had a factory in Naarden and some people in Vlaardingen from Unilever Research and Development, both in the Netherlands.

It was in the factory in Naarden, built just two years earlier, that Sierkstra saw an opportunity to reverse the downturn in income by using some of the factory's capacity for outside orders. 'We had orders from DSM, Unichema, Diosynth', he recalls. 'That triggered an ambition in us to move beyond the service segment we were in toward actually developing and producing our own products'.

In late 1999, Sierkstra and his team started exploring whether they could make that transition happen and could develop a business case for it. The fact that Unilever was also thinking about closing the factory in Naarden, despite the fact that it had cost NLG35 million (at the time) and had only been running for four years, added to the impetus to become independent and not waste that investment. They started by presenting a detailed business case to the R&D department under which BAC BV fell at the time. That division responded that their plans did not dovetail with Unilever's strategy. A year later, in late 2002, they were given a second chance to present their plan with the establishment of Unilever Ventures.

'Andrew Lane at Unilever Ventures liked the idea immediately', says Sierkstra. 'The alternative, after all, was to close the factory and see those patents go down the drain'. By approaching Sierkstra's business case as an opportunity, Unilever Ventures created the possibility of successfully cashing in on BAC BV. There was not so much a strategic interest for Unilever Ventures in investing, but there was a future beneficial financial interest.

While it still essentially remained part of Unilever, it also received money from Unilever Ventures. 'Our question was whether they would be able to acquire customers with their business idea', Coombs recalls. 'This meant they had to learn a new skill: selling. As they were scientists, not business development people, we helped them find Bruce Dawson. At some point, we decided that there was enough traction to actually form a company'.

The 'go' from Unilever Ventures set the spin-out process in motion, a process that eventually took two full years to complete. No fewer than 20 patents had to be transferred from the parent company, employment contracts had to be modified and outside funding needed to be arranged. 'When you create these ventures, you start to love them', Coombs explains. 'They are like your own children and you think they are perfect, and of course they might well not be. If you can't attract money into it, you've probably got a dog'. The internal spin-off was financed by Unilever Ventures for that initial period (2003–2005) and in early 2005 Sierkstra and his fellow director, Ingeborg van Gemeren, succeeded in finding two investors for BAC BV: Fleming Family & Partners and Stewart Newton.

For BAC BV then, 2005 was the moment of separation; it needed its own IT systems and patent agents and had to run entirely independently. There were two exceptions made to this uncoupling: payroll and the associated pension provisions. Sierkstra explains:

> The reason for this is that we needed the recommendation of the Works Council for the spin-out to occur. In essence, we decided at the time to say, 'We'll just stay in the Unilever pension fund; we're still a subsidiary of Unilever anyway'. But that also meant that you had to do your payroll through Unilever, so that everything could be processed properly.

The organizational structure for BAC BV is fairly simple. The management of the close corporation is made up of Sierkstra together with Ingeborg van Gemeren; they report directly to their Supervisory Board. That board consists of one representative from Unilever Ventures, an independent chairperson and one representative from Fleming on behalf of the VCs.

All told, the entire spin-out process took just about two years. One of the primary reasons for that long lead time was the complexities surrounding the patents. These had to be transferred from various Unilever groups, such as Port Sunlight and Colworth House, both in England. Although those other groups had developed and funded the patents, prising them away boiled down more to a political issue, rather than a financial one. The role played by Unilever Ventures was particularly valuable on this front. They were in a position to argue the case for establishing BAC with Unilever's top management and thus accomplish the patent transfer that was such a necessary part of that. 'In hindsight, it was a continuous process, in a way', says Sierkstra:

> You could call it a 'soft' spin-out, as we took two to three years to set up the company, taking care of what we needed to do to launch our products, to develop the products. And on 1 January 2005 we simply continued doing what we had already been doing in the years leading up to that.

Most of the capital investment they received in 2005 to create the spin-out was used to renovate the factory in Naarden. With the orders BAC BV already had from Unilever and third parties, they could then move on to selling the products. This kept the burn rate (or negative cash flow) relatively low, by biotechnology standards. The difficulty with BAC's business model is that it takes a very long time to get new customers to buy. They need to become acquainted with the technology, and once they understand it, they want proof. Then the customer needs all the work done for their specific activities. If they are going to take a new drug to the US Food and Drug Administration (FDA), they have to describe the manufacturing process, including defining the entire BAC process. 'That process can take three to four years from first point of engagement with BAC', explains Coombs:

> You will earn a little bit of money along the way, but not a lot, until you get to that approval level. The good bit is, once you're approved, and provided that the drug goes to market, you have locked in revenues, because it would require going all the way back to the FDA for re-approval.

So, it is an interesting business model, with very strong lock-in. The revenue stream is positively ensured for a 20-year period. Yet, while it is certainly interesting, it is also quite a long, slow-burn business model. 'We always thought that it was not going to be a three- or four-year investment. It was going to be a much longer investment. But progressively the business got more clients and built up its revenue stream and it has now reached the point that it's break-even', says Coombs.

From spin-out to exit

At some point, Unilever Ventures and Sierkstra knew that the business would need to be sold to someone to take it to the next stage. One of the things that will always hold back a business like BAC BV is the level of risk for the client. Sierkstra says:

> If you are a large company aiming to launch a new drug you want to be sure that the company you work with will still be around in 25 years. That means it would be reassuring for customers if instead of being a separate entity, BAC BV was a technology division in the portfolio of a big pharmaceutical service provider.

In 2010, the board of the company, on which all of the shareholders were represented, had concluded that once the company reached break-even, it made sense to sell it on the strength of its technology and locked-in revenues, rather than keep pushing it. Since then, Sierkstra and Van Gemeren's management team has been working to make that happen.

When it comes to selling off a spin-out there is a difference between strategic buyers and financial buyers. Financial buyers have a different aim than strategic buyers. Their focus is much more short term and therefore the price they are willing to pay is lower than that of a strategic buyer. So

Unilever Ventures' decision was to sell to a strategic buyer. As Coombs explains:

> At the start of a spin-out process, one of the questions we ask is: if we are successful in creating this business, will there be buyers for it when we get to the end? Because if the answer is yes, you can create a really nice business, but if there won't be any buyers, you better not start.

In the technology business, before people want to acquire a company, they often like to be that company's customer in some shape or form first. They really want to understand it, including any flaws. That makes it difficult to hide anything about the flaws in your technology from an acquirer. If you have a poor technology, it is very difficult to sell it. You only have a chance of selling a company if you have genuinely good technology that works. Another point of concern is how many potential buyers there will be. The more potential buyers there are who are strategically interested in the business, the better the price they will be willing to pay.

The sale process starts four or five years before the actual sale, by securing customers who might become acquirers in the future. As soon as one of those customers starts expressing interest in the technology, by, for instance, trying to lock out other customers through a commercial agreement (the so-called bear hug), the spin-out needs to examine whether it is a good moment to sell. A lot of the value in a company being sold is thus achieved through the terms and conditions of the commercial agreements they have reached in previous years; termination clauses and scope clauses have a huge effect on the value of a company in a final exit.

As soon as one interested party is found, it is customary to have quiet conversations with two or three other acquirers, explaining the company's wish to sell. As Coombs explains:

> You tend to keep it quiet because the worst thing that can happen when you try to sell is failing to do so. That happened to BAC two years ago. The process was aborted because the best bid was too low. We had to take BAC back off the market for 18 months. We couldn't just go back and try again.

Unilever Ventures sold BAC in January 2013 to Life Technologies, a US company. The main draws for the buyer were the patents held by BAC BV and the fact that BAC's products were accepted by the biopharmaceutical community as being excellent products for the purification of biopharmaceuticals. This will enable Life Technologies to use the technology to put more new products onto the market. Sierkstra says:

> Life Technologies is an excellent takeover entity. And I think that they will benefit tremendously from our technology in not only the field we currently operate in, but also a few entirely different application areas that they will be able to exploit and we couldn't, simply because we had too little know-how, though we did have the technology fit.

The plant and the people will remain in the Netherlands, since it is too expensive to relocate, but the new company will have the go-to-market capability of a US corporation. For Sierkstra and Van Gemeren, it means they will become employees at Life Technologies. It is still unknown what the organizational form will be after the takeover. BAC BV could continue to operate as an independent organization under Life Technologies or it could be incorporated into a new organization. 'It is incredibly exciting', exclaims Sierkstra. 'It is also really fun to have experienced the whole process: from spin-out to exit. It was incredibly interesting. And this last bit is definitely also tremendously fun and very educational. I'm pretty curious, too, about where we'll end up'.

Four operational elements in the venture process

There are four operational elements that play a role in the venturing process. The first is organization: how are the venturing endeavours to be organized within the company? And is a model being used to streamline the process? The second concerns the portfolio: how will the venture company align its venture activities with the strategy of the parent company? The composition of the venture teams is the third element: do the people involved in the venturing organization require specific competencies? How do you find these people? And, more importantly, how do you retain them for longer periods of time, considering that the venturing process can often take eight to ten years? The final element concerns the structure for the connection between the venture and the parent company. How can they remain in touch without obstructing one another in terms of achieving their goals? Each of these elements will be discussed in the following paragraphs.

Model

'When you are running a company, it is what you do', Coombs says. 'So the board of that company is thinking on a weekly basis about the route forward. What are my key tasks? What risks do I have to mitigate and what's the cash requirement for that? There's a constant dialogue going on at the board level of a company'.

In his organization, ventures are organized more along the lines of a venture capital fund. Coombs says:

> Basically, what we are saying is: if there's bad news, we want to hear about it as soon as possible, and not at the end of a stage when we need to decide whether the next stage is a go or no-go. When we do hear about it, the decision as to what to do now, we are going to take that right away. That's the problem with stage gating; every time projects start looking a bit dodgy, the right thing to do is usually shut them down immediately. But the people who are running the project will try in every possible way to keep it alive.

Portfolio management

Most venture companies work with so-called portfolio management to create focus on the areas that need strategic development. So, too, Unilever Ventures. In order to create strategic alignment between parent and subsidiary, Unilever has agreed with Unilever Ventures to focus on four practical areas for which they are most likely to tick the strategic box if they find investments: that is, (1) digital marketing, (2) refreshment, (3) personal care and (4) sustainability. 'What we do is we say, "All our investments need to be in one of those four areas"', according to Coombs.

Composing a venture team

Apart from the importance of how the decision-making is structured within the venture business, having the right people on your team – and retaining them – is quite essential as well. Unilever Ventures has designed a structure that allows them to both recruit from the venture capital or private equity world and keep the team together over a longer period of time. As Coombs says:

> The conclusion you come to, when you go through the analyses, is that you need to have an incentive arrangement that is the same as, or very similar to, the incentive arrangement you have in the venture capital world, where it's normal that at the top the management of the fund would stay together for 10 to 15 years.

They take a seat on the boards of the ventures they invest in. Approximately 70 per cent of their time is spent running the companies they have already invested in; the other 30 per cent is about investing in new businesses. His team consists of three directors on the investment committee; four investment directors, who will serve as directors on company boards; and two junior associates. So, the actual investment staff is nine people. They also have a support team of three finance people. 'There it is very much about whether they have the right strategy; whether they have the right financing; and whether they have the right people', he adds.

When you look at BAC BV, you realize that they actually already had their team in place when they were designated a spin-out under the Unilever Ventures programme, so it did not need to be assembled separately. In the course of spinning out the business, the people who made up that team turned out to be suited to the roles they had to fill. It is true that they also brought in new people along the way to fill out the organization. 'We had to set up a mini-organization consisting of manufacturing, quality assurance, quality control, finance, R&D and applications', says Sierkstra:

> The R&D and applications we had. The manufacturing we had. But our Quality Assurance/Quality Control position was weak and we didn't have a Finance position, so we picked up those two. We also pretty much do our own HR. When you are a small, lean organization, it's not too involved. It was only when it concerned something like an employment contract that we might run it back through Unilever, since the pensions were also tied in to that.

Connection to the parent company

The Unilever Ventures office is located in Central London, approximately two miles from the parent company's office. This was done on purpose, as it gives Unilever Ventures the opportunity to present themselves as an entrepreneurial organization to the external partners with whom they interact. 'Internally, we structure in Unilever's categories and we organize an interface with Unilever very well', says Coombs. 'I have a Unilever business card; I have a Unilever e-mail address, so I can network back in. We have some distance, because in the world of entrepreneurs, they prefer to come in here'.

Unilever Ventures is, in effect, a management company within Unilever that advises the parent company about investments of strategic interest. The relationship between BAC BV and Unilever Ventures is somewhat different. In that case, Unilever Ventures is basically a shareholder in BAC BV, and their interest is a financial one: to lead the spin-out toward the exit stage as successfully as possible in order to obtain the best possible return. Sierkstra and his team were prompted, in the beginning, to develop their own business plan because of changes in Unilever's strategic path. The fact that biotechnology units were being sold off offered BAC BV an opportunity to further pursue its business as a Unilever spin-out. Unilever purchases only very small volumes from BAC BV, so in that sense the strategic relationship between the two parties is limited in scope.

How to breed success

With the recent successful spin-out of BAC BV, the question that arises is: how do you create a successful venture? In Coombs's experience, there are two difficulties to counter when dealing with ventures. The first is knowing when to pull the plug. When a business hits a rough patch and is missing its targets, when do you decide to stop investing, since no company goes nice and smoothly from start-up to success? 'Whenever you are in the trough, the natural instinct is to cut your losses', Coombs says. 'Everyone says about venture capital: they are really good and when things don't go right, then they cut. But if every time one of our companies missed its targets, we killed it, we would have nothing left in that portfolio. Every single one we would have killed'.

The second difficulty concerns people: knowing when to let somebody go. 'And by somebody, it's nearly always the CEO or that kind of key director you keep using as a business development director', Coombs points out. 'Knowing when to part company is, again, really difficult. And actually, the conclusion we come to every time we've analysed our performance on this is: we are always too slow'. It is especially a difficult decision to make since the person who needs to be removed from the venture is the one who created the business. It is not like a normal job for them and it is practically impossible to find a suitable replacement. When it goes wrong, it is often due to the fact that the CEO does not have the strategic view necessary to get the business started or does not have the implementation skills.

The way these venture processes are managed does not differ much from one to another, even if the venture itself might have a more financial, rather than strategic, aim. 'We will do some things that are financial but not strategic, like spinning out and exiting BAC BV', Coombs points out. And that is something it did successfully in January 2013, when Life Technologies purchased BAC BV. Now a new challenge lies ahead for Sierkstra and his team: the spinning in of BAC BV at the new parent company.

4

Document Services Valley: a lifeline for the printing industry?

Jessica van den Bosch and Stijn van den Hoogen

After a 35-year career at Océ, Jan Verschaeren knows the company inside and out. When it was acquired by Canon in 2009, it was only logical then that he was asked to head the Document Printing business unit as its executive vice president. That was the first business unit to be integrated into the Canon organization. And once that process was complete, mid-2012, he was asked to tackle one last project before finally retiring: to design Document Services Valley (DSV).

Océ started as a family business in 1877, when Lodewijk van der Grinten, a pharmacist by trade, developed a dye for colouring margarine yellow like butter before it was sold onto the market. Thirty years later, one of Van der Grinten's descendants decided to deploy that dye expertise in his own research into blueprint materials. By 1927 the company had successfully applied for a patent on its semi-dry diazo process, a new technology that had the advantage of being able to produce a positive instead of a negative image. By the mid-twentieth century, the electrostatic copying machines that would make Océ big were introduced onto the market. And in 1996 the company entered the printing market with its takeover of the printing division of Siemens Nixdorf. Then, as the market came under intense, increasing pressure, Océ decided to focus on the niche markets of large-format and large-volume copiers.

In 2009 Canon announced plans to acquire Océ. Canon, which also has digital and video cameras in its portfolio of products, in addition to printers, copiers and scanners, was primarily interested in Océ because of the company's know-how and creativity. Moreover, the takeover would make Canon the world's largest supplier in the printing industry.

Innovation at Océ

Océ adopted a business unit structure for its organization in the late 1970s and has always had three to four business units in operation since then, each focused on a particular market. 'For instance', explains Verschaeren, 'my former business unit, Document Printing, targeted primarily the corporate market. A second business unit was aimed at serving the technical documents market with equipment for "large-format drawings". And the third business unit, in Germany, targeted the high-volume printing market, like for printing newspapers or bank statements'. In addition to these business units focused on printers, Océ had a fourth business unit, called Business Services, which provided in-house document services such as managing print and mail rooms for clients. Each unit was responsible for formulating its own strategy, conducting its own R&D and developing innovations. The entire product innovation process, production, engineering, and so on, was therefore carried out in each business unit. 'The strategic thinking and translating that into products and services, that is what the business units did', says Verschaeren.

Also as far back as the late 1970s, Océ was already working on the Future Office concept. At the time, this was mostly related to transitioning from copying to printing. The rise of the paperless office followed some time afterward, leading Océ, about midway through the 2000s, to think that it needed to come up with new printing solutions and services to counterbalance any subsequent decline in printing volumes. With the company's vast store of knowledge in the area of document management, such initiatives could easily result in new business. It would require, however, a different kind of knowledge and expertise than what was needed to develop new printers. And that is how the idea for Document Services Valley originated back in 2007, during the company's 130-year anniversary.

Document Services Valley

Huib Adriaans joined Océ in 2010 while doing his final thesis project on corporate venturing. He was charged with exploring the possibilities for setting up a structured corporate venturing organization and strategy within Océ. At the time, Océ already had two ventures under its umbrella. These had originally formed more or less spontaneously but had made the company realize that more opportunities for new products and services were probably lying in wait, ready for someone to pick up and run with. Add to that the fact that the printing industry was under considerable pressure as a result of widespread digitalization – Canon's takeover of Océ at that time only served to underscore the point. From that perspective, corporate venturing offered an excellent way of structuring innovation within the company, were it not for the fact that as a result of the takeover, all of the emphasis had turned to integrating the two companies. Nevertheless, this did not diminish the strategic interest for Océ of investing in innovation. Document Services Valley presented an alternative way of achieving that.

The essence of document services is to develop new service ideas in the area of document and information management that do not necessarily involve a printer. Since services are best developed with customer input, which requires a different kind of knowledge than is needed when developing hardware, the company decided to pursue this project through open innovation. In 2009 it embarked on a path to seek government subsidies that eventually landed it considerable funding for the project, with Océ being one of the promoters, along with the Dutch Ministry of Economic Affairs and the Dutch Province of Limburg. Joining Océ as knowledge partners and co-founders were Maastricht University and Exser, a private–public group promoting service innovation. Document Services Valley was launched on 1 January 2011 and Adriaans started working as a business developer there.

The goal of Document Services Valley was to use the allocated subsidy within two years to help build the largest possible relevant network of companies working in the field of document services, to help as many companies as possible with feasible ideas become commercially successful. 'But also to create an environment, a physical environment, where those companies were welcome', Adriaans points out. Océ, as co-promoter, would naturally also benefit because these kinds of innovative start-ups would provide a clear idea of where the market for document services was headed. This would yield insight into future trends and developments of interest to a company such as Océ, especially in a tight market environment, and might also pave the way for possibly working together with these companies, although that was certainly not the original intent of the project.

The Document Services Valley team was made up of three business developers who were responsible for attracting and guiding the innovative companies, and one person who was in charge of establishing a network of suppliers for services, such as app designers, legal advisors and market researchers. The team also had its own marketing communications specialist on board to provide virtual support for the network's formation through social media and other means. The management consisted primarily of representatives from the prime movers behind the subsidy request, but the operational team basically comprised five people. Adriaans says:

> All of the members of the team came from Océ and were being seconded. There were two team members from R&D, one from the Communications department, one from Human Resources, and one came from the Corporate Public Affairs department – they were the ones that submitted the subsidy request. So, it was actually a very diverse team, made up of people from various backgrounds.

Structure and organization

With the subsidy locked in and the idea in their hands, the team had to get down to business. The first couple of months were devoted to finding the best way to go about that. Adriaans explains:

> You meet with a couple of companies, enterprising companies. Then you look at how you can help them. In the end, we decided to develop a structure under which the greatest share of the subsidy money was made directly available to entrepreneurs with innovative ideas in the area of document services.

The word 'document' here was given the broadest possible meaning, as a carrier of information. That meant that anything to do with creating, processing, storing, managing or publishing information was part and parcel of the document services domain. 'Then you immediately have a tremendously broad domain, but you can also more easily generate mass. We then started searching for innovative companies in that domain to invest the €800 000 subsidy in', Adriaans explains.

A foundation was formed to properly manage the subsidy funds. Given Océ's involvement, this was also necessary to ensure that the subsidy was not seen as some form of state support. The board of the foundation was made up of stakeholders from the parties that had requested the subsidy. One of the board members proposed that the support and funding process be divided into three stages, with the maximum allotted amount of subsidy money per company, €22 500, also being divided into three portions of €7 500 each. That was the inception of the so-called Programme for Acceleration of (Document) Services Innovation (PADSI) for which companies could apply (see Figure 4.2 below). Adriaans explains:

> The idea behind it was that an entrepreneur could start by describing his or her business idea in one or two pages: what is the company structure; what does the market look like (in other words, what are the problems and opportunities); what is our idea; what's innovative about it; and what kind of help will we need to develop it? You might, for instance, have a real techie who needs support in the area of market research or a commercial person looking for someone to help them build an app. Our underlying idea behind this approach was: what if instead of paying out the subsidy money ahead of time, we agreed to reimburse costs incurred? Then we could see right off whether or not we were dealing with entrepreneurship at work. In other words, is someone prepared to invest their own money ahead of time and receive some subsidy back from us afterwards?

And it is a strategy that fits in well with the notion of open innovation: working together to develop things is faster and better than trying to go it alone. One of the ventures they invested in was QBengo.

QBengo: find and be found

QBengo sprung from the brain of Remon van der Heide. A few years ago, he was at a networking event full of attendees who could potentially prove very useful for him to know. That led him to think about how great it would be if you could see either before or during such an occasion which of the people would be worthwhile meeting – which contacts would bring you the greatest added value in the limited time you had to meet with them and exchange knowledge.

With the rise of smartphones and resultant growth in applications, that idea became a real possibility. He developed his business idea further into an actual app and quickly found the needed incubation funds, which he used to make a pilot version and test it with the launching customer, Eindhoven University of Technology (TU/e). Van der Heide is now about to roll out the QBengo app onto the market. The first major presentation of the product will occur in conjunction with a conference organizer early next year.

QBengo allows everyone entering a particular location, such as a networking or other kind of event, to download the app onto his or her smartphone. Based on your personal objectives for the day, the app then directs you to the people or locations you want to meet or visit. You might also, for instance, attach your LinkedIn or Facebook profile so that you are also introducing your own profile to connect with people of interest to you. Find and be found. Van der Heide explains:

> As soon as you click on the search button you get an overview on your phone of the ten best matches for you out of all of the users in attendance. You can then click on each of these results to learn more about the people. When I send a request to the highest-ranked person shown in my overview of people from my initial search, that person can accept or decline. Being declined is not fun, but if my request is accepted, it means that person also knows who he is going to be talking to. So, the ice is already broken on either side. You are then each guided to a place to meet through your phone's navigation system. And since we include a current profile with a photo, there is a good chance I will recognize the person I'm meeting. That's what it's really about.

For the moment, the primary focus for QBengo is on large-scale institutions, universities and trade shows, although talks are also being held with hospitals, theme parks and retailers. The approach for now revolves around focusing the marketing efforts and introducing the app in certain sectors. Once those introductions are successful, the number of sectors can easily be broadened. The app is a generic model that can be customized for the client. Moreover, it can be self-operated through a licensing model, so that the client could manage any modifications of a temporary or permanent nature that might be needed.

The application finds wide acceptance because of its underlying business model. It is obviously in the best interests of the organizers of large events to ensure that participants get the most out of their visit. And there is the added benefit of being able to combine the app with relevant advertising content. As Van der Heide says:

What they do now is hand out maps of the event site to people as they come in, showing where all the stands are located, with the logos of the vendors and sponsors on the back, whereas our app allows organizers to share targeted information with the client that is relevant to him or her.

That makes the whole experience much more efficient and meaningful for both organizers and participants. After all, then the vendors know that only people who are truly interested in their product or service will be visiting their stand. And the impact of the advertising will be much more direct than with a logo on the back of a map. 'It's really about the pay-back models', he adds, 'through which I allow clients to share in the revenue that can be generated on top of the traditional revenue stream. That is especially interesting for conventions'.

QBengo was one of the 86 companies included in the first phase of the Document Services Valley programme. The added value of being in that programme for Van der Heide came from not just the bit of financing he received, but also, more importantly, the support from the business developers and the new network that evolved from that. For Document Services Valley, QBengo is a classic example of how things will change in the future: no more big maps that need to be specially printed for events but a navigating app that brings people together.

QBengo has now completed all three phases of the current programme. The new programme that started 1 June 2013 recently launched a fourth phase, for which Van der Heide once again made a proposal, aimed at acquiring growth capital. He concludes:

The growth really could occur very quickly. The biggest combinations, of course, are in China: that's where I can find the people I need, corresponding to the demand that we create here. So we have to devote some resources to marketing but it must be precisely targeted. Not so much for distributing the application, because I believe it will catch on very quickly through the internet, but more to boost awareness of my company and the possibilities our product has to offer.

Four operational elements in the venture process

So, what kind of model does DSV use in order to create ventures? Do they have a portfolio that offers them support in focusing on the right strategic pathway? How do they make sure they have the right team members on board? And how have they organized the alignment with the parent company?

The model

Once they had a brief written description of the business idea, the business developers got down to work. They considered whether the idea fit in the document services domain, was truly innovative in terms of presenting an alternative to existing solutions and had been submitted by a true entrepreneur. If these three criteria were met, the business developers gave the entrepreneur the go-ahead to start on the first stage of development. Of more than 140 ideas submitted, 86 were eventually taken to Phase 1 and received funding.

In the beginning, the business developers worked individually in interfacing with the entrepreneurs but they soon started to team up. 'There were actually two reasons for that', Adriaans explains. 'First off, three people know more than one, but also for sharing knowledge, knowing what the others were working on or what kinds of companies they had in their portfolio'. This also allowed them to make connections between the companies much more easily. Since everyone was working in the area of document services, there was always some common ground.

The first phase involved exploring how feasible the concept was (both technically and commercially). The findings at that stage were meant to yield insight that the entrepreneur could use to differentiate his or her product or service from those of others and acquire paying customers. That insight also helped him or her formulate a solid proposal. 'The entrepreneurs then pitched their proposals to the foundation board, which decided go or no-go for proceeding to the next, the second, phase', says Adriaans. 'What we do in Phase 2 is actually test your concept with a paying customer in a pilot'.

Originally, the foundation board used the same three criteria to evaluate the proposals that the business developers had in the previous phase, but after a while it became clear that the process should be professionalized. So, they drew up a form with criteria that could be evaluated on a scale of one to five. Meanwhile, the business developers started advising the entrepreneurs to seek their first customer before giving the pitch for progressing to the second stage. Adriaans points out:

> If you can tell the committee 'This is my proposal and I have found a company that believes in it and wants to test it out with me', then that obviously increases your chances of making it to the next level. If the board has any reservations, you can at least point to the fact that one customer, in any event, believes in it. Then the board is more inclined to say, 'Okay, let's see how it does in the next phase'.

Figure 4.1 illustrates the DSV development funnel (see Preface).

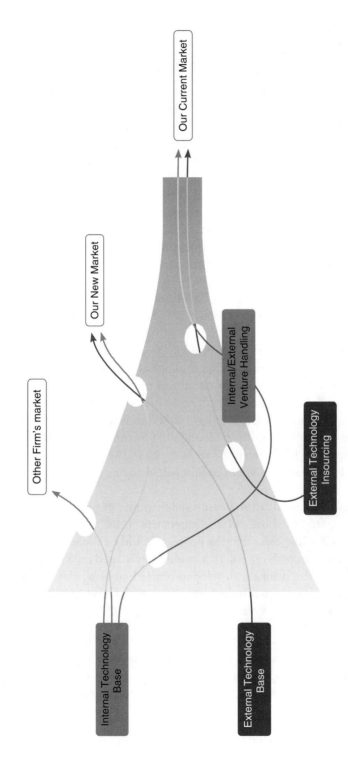

Figure 4.1 DSV development funnel

Of the 86 companies that reached Phase 1, 43 have currently progressed to Phase 2. That second stage revolves primarily around implementing the pilot project and eventually developing the service into a market-ready product. To prepare the entrepreneurs for promoting their product, pitch coaching sessions are held in which they present test pitches. The entrepreneurs can avail themselves of a pitch protocol developed by the business developers to get ready for these.

The final stage in the process concerns scaling up to three or more customers. Even with a customer already in the pocket, that still means pulling in at least another two. Naturally, the end goal depends on the entrepreneur's venture: having three customers buy an app is an entirely different matter than winning three sizable service contracts.

To move up from Phase 2 to Phase 3, the entrepreneur must once again pitch his or her proposal to the foundation board. That pitch is expected to include a brief summary of the entrepreneur's experience with the pilot and any subsequent developments, as well as a description of potential areas for improvement. Adriaans explains:

> The ultimate conclusion in that pitch should obviously be, 'Yes, I have a successful venture. I've already tested it with one customer, in any case, and I know what I need to do, both in terms of the service itself and financially, to scale it up. So, I am ready for Phase 3'.

Of the 43 companies that reached Phase 2, ten have since moved on to Phase 3 (Figure 4.2). Several others of the remaining 33 enterprises are also expected to proceed to the third stage. The business developers never set deadlines for the businesses, although that is common practice with many other incubators. 'We tended to leave it up to the entrepreneurs themselves. Of course, we mentioned that it would be first come, first served, primarily to encourage them to keep up the momentum', says Adriaans.

Portfolio

When Document Services Valley was launched in September 2011, the immediate focus was on building a network of relevant entrepreneurs and businesses for the purpose of bringing in as many feasible ideas as possible in the area of document services. There was no other focus at the time, and on top of that, the notion of a 'document' had been very broadly defined as a 'carrier of information'. The first acquisitions resulted from a great many meetings with local agencies, such as the Limburg Development Company

Programme for Acceleration of (Document) Services Innovation (PADSI)

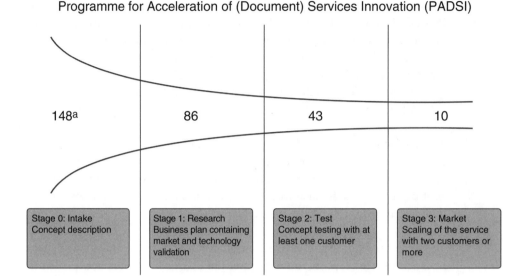

| 148a | 86 | 43 | 10 |

Stage 0: Intake	Stage 1: Research	Stage 2: Test	Stage 3: Market
Concept description	Business plan containing market and technology validation	Concept testing with at least one customer	Scaling of the service with two customers or more

Note: a. Cumulative number of companies involved in the Programme. The other figures are numbers of companies involved at each stage.

Figure 4.2 Programme for Acceleration of (Document) Services Innovation (DSV stage gates)

LIOF, North Brabant Development Agency BOM and various Chambers of Commerce, along with visits to field-specific events and conferences, as well as self-initiated monthly networking cocktail parties and workshops. 'With all these efforts, we quickly – by spring of 2012 – had some 30 to 35 interested companies', says Adriaans. 'And then you saw the network effect play out, the flywheel just took off. But this did produce a rather unstructured portfolio'.

The advantage of this strategy is that it produces a diverse portfolio; the disadvantage is that there is no strategic line feeding into the strategy of the parent organization, Canon. Under the new funding round, this is expected to be more the direction the project takes, in part because Canon has indicated that it would like to include the camera business in this incubator initiative. Adriaans points out:

> The idea is that the business developers will be in charge of one or two domains and also become more active in acquisitions for their domains. But that doesn't mean you should immediately reject everything that falls outside those parameters, because then you put the blinders back on and start thinking with a corporate mindset. Our very success was due to the fact that our environment was very open

and we allowed in a great many ideas. They might not all have been appropriate to take straight to Océ or Canon, but they were all still based on an interesting concept.

Ideas do not need to fit instantly into today's Canon portfolio. It is much more valuable to see how new concepts, technologies and/or business models might affect the future of that portfolio.

By working more from a portfolio perspective, the business developers can also try to exercise more control over the lead-in times of the start-ups they are supervising. That way they can better manage the number of companies they have under them at each stage and thus ensure that they have enough offerings in the pipeline. That is especially important for the parent company and stakeholders, to show that not only will you be generating returns in the long term, but also there are more immediate-term profits. There is, however, a risk that as the business developers aim for financial results, they will unconsciously stake their resources on their pet projects. 'You obviously want to give everyone the same chance. But it's true that you have a few that you suspect or know could be especially interesting for Canon or other investors. That plays a role, unconsciously, but on the other hand, it's also about the people who actively approach you', Adriaans points out.

The impact of Document Services Valley on Canon

There is great strategic interest in continuing to pursue Document Services Valley now that the present funding has been spent. The access to new business opportunities has been well demonstrated to Canon, as a co-promoter, over the past two years. One example of this is the company EuMediaNet. They develop interactive monitor networks that can be installed in cities and will broadcast a particular advertising message based on who is passing by. While that might, at first glance, appear to be far removed from Canon's operations, Adriaans explains just how pertinent for the present business model it actually is:

All those places where interactive screens now hang, those used to be billboards printed by the 'large-format' division. Paper media is being gradually replaced with digital applications and that is exactly what we need to be prepared for. With the start-ups that we support through Document Services Valley, we can demonstrate this and help Canon see that.

Now that the subsidy has been spent, Document Services Valley has been looking into ways of structuring and financing the project's continuation, particularly for the companies that are in Phase 2 or recently entered Phase 3, which mostly need funding. Document Services Valley is presently structured as a foundation, with the participation of Maastricht University and Exser (through its 'Peaks in the Delta' programme) alongside Canon. Canon plans to continue investing, as does the Province of Limburg.

As the project's director, Verschaeren would like to involve two other corporate incubators in the initiative, in order to bring in more objective external knowledge that could be useful for the incubators. Because information management is such a broad field, it overlaps with many other industries that find themselves in similar situations, such as the telecom industry. By involving corporates from those industries, you boost the Valley's level of knowledge and increase your appeal for other companies. Verschaeren is also searching for Venture Capitalists as a way to attract funding for innovative companies in the long term. While a €22 500 allowance is certainly a welcome endowment for these companies, the level of investment needed once you start developing and scaling up your service is much greater. To bring all these variables into harmony, he is now in the process of forming a limited liability company (Dutch BV) to operate under the control of the foundation. This will also open up the possibility, down the line, of acquiring shares in the companies, so that the organization shifts from grant-based funding to a professional funding structure with its own earnings model.

The new company will have a budget of another €800 000 available for innovative entrepreneurs when it is formed. Verschaeren plans to use this to establish several eco-environments: for product information, for imaging and for printing in corporate worlds. Establishing those eco-environments will require business developers to proactively acquire entities and find other corporates in a given domain. The incubatees/companies that are brought in then also need to be coached with knowledge and expertise. It is essential, in this, that that knowledge and expertise does not come exclusively from Canon, to prevent falling back on simply manufacturing more printers, hence the significance of the partnership with other corporate incubators in the initiative.

For the time being, Verschaeren and his team can develop projects through Document Services Valley to advance innovations that align with Canon's business strategy but they cannot force any acquisitions or partnerships. By setting up a limited liability company under the foundation, however, and appointing members to its supervisory board and securing financial support from Canon's business units, you can consolidate the bond between parent company and incubator.

'The trick is to get that critical mass going and to find ways of tapping into new innovative chances and opportunities', says Verschaeren. Stressing the financial commitment on the part of the business units is currently triggering that momentum, by reiterating at every public get-together just how important Document Services Valley is. 'Hopefully', he continues, 'we can quickly get past this rather awkward, labour-intensive stage for these sorts of things. Because it would, of course, be very nice if some of the products we're making here, if some of those eventually carried a Canon label, too'. By introducing a fourth phase in this incubator approach, for instance, companies with a need for financing could be more easily connected to the right people. This would not necessarily have to evolve into a partnership between the start-ups and Canon, but could rather merely constitute a financial interest for Canon in the new business.

Team composition

The composition of the team at the time was not dictated by a focus on particular competencies, but was more of a logical grouping of interested staff who thought it would be fun to help shape this project. Adriaans recalls:

> When I look back at how we started on this as a team, then I think our strength was that we were all young. Young people who knew the company well but weren't stuck in that culture of 'printer think', just employees who were ambitious, prepared to help out those entrepreneurs.

In an audit of the factors in the success of the Document Services Valley project, the commitment of its business developers was named the single greatest added value. This included their ability to ask the right questions and think along conceptual lines and openness in reviewing the ideas submitted. But they also complemented one another nicely as a team, with different ages, backgrounds and levels of experience represented. 'In the end, it boils down to having a certain degree of entrepreneurialism – not being an entrepreneur, but being entrepreneurial', Adriaans adds.

Now that the project has a business-based second act with the formation of a limited liability company, the question arises as to whether there will be a greater focus on the team composition, whether competencies will become a bigger issue.

The next stage for Document Services Valley

Document Services Valley's greatest strength is that it has produced an incredible leap in knowledge in the field of document and information management and everything related to that. 'You can already see that the printing world is no longer growing. At most, Canon might be able to push another few competitors out of the market, but then there are just fewer of you sharing that shrinking pie', says Verschaeren.

In that atmosphere, the number of ideas that Document Services Valley brought in and developed over the past two years attracted growing interest on the part of parent company Canon. 'Those kinds of numbers are not the kind Canon could have achieved on its own by looking internally for new ideas', Adriaans points out. 'And since we left the field so open, we also added some companies that might not be interesting today or tomorrow, but do provide an impression of where things are headed in the future'. With the establishment of the limited liability company in June 2013, a whole new organization is being created and with it new opportunities. It is difficult to predict how these will all play out for Canon.

In the new PADSI round that also started in June 2013, the focus has shifted from subsidy to participation. The process remains the same though: three phases to help entrepreneurs get from idea to market and a fourth phase that has been added for the event that a company receives an investment at an investor day. The amounts, however, have changed: €2500 in Phase 1 and €7500 in Phase 2, again as an allowance to reimburse costs incurred. In Phase 3 a company receives a €15 000 investment from Document Services Valley. In return for this support, the Incubator BV asks for a 6 per cent equity stake in each company that enters Phase 2. This way there is a commitment from both parties to turn the idea into a great success. And once successful, both parties benefit. The incubator can then use the money raised from an exit to invest again in new companies. This way a revolving fund is created to support PADSI.

5

Innovation projects and venturing at Rabobank: creating a new dynamic

Jessica van den Bosch and Victor Gilsing

Michael Dooijes joined Rabobank in 2007. As a former international relationship manager who worked abroad for many years, and as a stockbroker with 20 years of experience in Wholesale and Retail Financial Services, in 2011 he was given responsibility for strategy and innovation at the commercial bank business arm of Rabobank Nederland. The financial world is not typically known for its innovation, but it is currently undergoing a sea change. The widespread digitization that has occurred has caused many outsiders to adopt a new view of the financial sector's business model. Traditional banking has become a commodity, with young new companies developing related services for offering customers more options. This has been dubbed the FinTech industry: radical innovations that link technological applications to the banking business model.

To some extent, these constitute a threat to the relationship a bank has with its customers; the insertion of other parties with services of interest to the consumer distances the bank from its customers. This has necessitated a change of culture within the banking sector. But the trend can also be viewed as an opportunity. By capitalizing on these developments as a bank, you can add value to your relationship with your customers. That will require, of course, embracing open innovation in terms of partnering with other, outside, parties to achieve innovation.

'The trick is to work more closely with start-ups because they need us as much as we need them', says Harrie Vollaard, head of innovation at Rabobank's IT company:

> There is inevitably a win-win situation to be had, the only question is: how are you going to organize it? Because the problem right now is that if a start-up comes to us and says, 'We want to work with Rabobank', that's a very difficult proposition for Rabobank. The bank has a reputation to uphold. It looks at the start-up and thinks, 'The risk is extremely high; [the company] is untested. Do we want to associate ourselves with that?' So you have to look for a way to still get it done anyway.

Structure and organization

The Strategy and Innovation department is independently run but falls under the Product Management team. A conscious decision was made not to position it as a separate unit outside the parent organization. Dooijes says:

> I like being so close to the business, so that I know what's happening in the very near term and what my colleagues are struggling with. That way I can help them understand what is going on more quickly. We are very good at today's business, it's

something we all do, but radical innovation . . . well, that's the piece I supply; that's more for the longer term.

Dooijes' sole resource from his department is an FTE (full-time equivalent) budget. All ideas must be presented to the innovation board, made up of a handful of Rabobank Nederland directors. He explains:

> Those five directors set the course, have ultimate responsibility and report directly to the Executive Board. They form the innovation board for me to present my ideas to. That is where we either get approval or not. If it involves a really big idea, such as a takeover, then I have to go straight to the Executive Board.

He works closely with Vollaard, who runs the Innovation department in Rabobank's IT business unit. That department originated with the rise of internet banking, about ten years ago. Vollaard points out:

> That was when people realized you could do more with IT than simply optimizing back office processes, that you could mobilize it to do something more for your customers, in this case in terms of distribution channels. IT was always playing catch up. Whenever there was a demand, our lack of know-how and expertise became apparent, and we would have to hurry up and supply it. I started there all by myself and now we have seven people working here.

Vollaard and Dooijes are working together to introduce truly radical innovations at Rabobank. Because of the bank's legacy as a cooperative bank, a conscious decision was made not to create a separate staff group, but to instead keep the innovation activities as close as possible to the line departments. The advantage of this is that any innovation is closely aligned with the parent company's needs, but the disadvantage is that innovations are being pursued at many levels, making it essential that those initiatives be shared and clearly communicated.

In essence, there are multiple Innovation departments or individuals that deal with innovation at the bank, what Vollaard and Dooijes describe as so-called pockets of innovation. One example is Teckle, a service at Rabobank Eindhoven that provides support to beginning entrepreneurs. Since Rabobank is a cooperative bank, the internal organizational structure is relatively complicated. Each individual bank is considered an independent part of the cooperative. The trick is bringing together all those different pockets of innovation. Vollaard says:

> We have some standard activities in which we all join together to take coordinated action, such as the annual trend analysis. That provides focus. We also hold

regular meetings and meet individually at the project level. The advantage of that is that after a few meetings you establish a relationship and people aren't afraid to approach one another. That does away with the need to constantly get together in formal meetings. The ultimate goal is for us to bring the outside world in with our innovative activities. What is going on with our customers and where should we be directing our efforts?

Rabobank's cooperative structure therefore does not immediately lend itself to the establishment of an independent venture organization. Dooijes explains:

> To start with there is, in point of fact, no parent company because the organization is built up out of local banks. So, you need to carefully assess what you want to link a venture organization to. It is precisely because of that organizational structure that you have to situate the innovation as closely as possible to the line organization.

Nevertheless, the methods these two gentlemen employ are comparable to those of external venturing, in the sense of investing in strategically interesting start-ups like MyOrder.

MyOrder

Thomas Brinkman is now 29 years old. In 2008 he received his Bachelor of Engineering (IT) from the Hanze University of Applied Sciences in Groningen, with a final project based on an idea that formed the seed of MyOrder. That idea originated, as befitting any good student, at a café. While waiting for his beer, Brinkman thought how ideal it would be if you could order and pay for your beer with your phone. 'It's also much more efficient for the business owner', he exclaims, 'because instead of having to bring you the menu, take your order, serve your order and bring you the bill, he now just has to serve the order'.

He thought it was such a promising idea that, upon graduating, he established MyOrder and started turning it into reality. He went looking for tech guys to help him program an app and investors willing to provide financing. After many pitches and presentations, he eventually found an IT company eager to do more with innovation. Together they set up a limited liability company (BV) and started the business. Along the way, a third party joined them: Eijsink, a Dutch supplier of point of sale (POS) and cash register systems. Brinkman says:

When you're working in the food industry trying to get cafés to sign up with MyOrder, you soon realize you're going to need a strategic partner in order to take it big quickly. And I noticed that it was the cash register suppliers in that industry who occupied a dominant position in the supply chain. We linked the two together. Eijsink has 20 per cent to 30 per cent of the food industry market as customers for its POS systems, making them the perfect partner to help us ramp up our roll out in the food industry and ensure that, with a partner like that, we attained even broader adoption.

Working in the food industry target group, Brinkman also came into contact with movie theatre (cinema) owners: all those long lines at the ticket windows and a lot of cash payments. It was the ideal expansion market for MyOrder. The menu used in the app for the food industry was replaced with theatre movie listings. Delivery restaurants followed the movie theatres and thus the applications kept expanding. As Brinkman points out:

At a certain point, you realize that you're actually creating a platform that is becoming more and more relevant to the consumer the more you can offer on it. Then we started rushing to make the MyOrder platform as relevant as possible to consumers. We already had everything in Groningen hooked up: bars, restaurants, cafés, movie theatres, hairdressers, tanning salons . . . And then you also saw how students were using it in more and more places.

At the time, Rabobank was working on enabling mobile payments but this was based more on a system in which a debit card had to be held up to a terminal to make the payment. The system MyOrder uses is remote payments (MiniTix, iDEAL, PayPal, CreditCard), in which you can make the payment from your touch screen and do not have to use your debit card. The main advantage of that is that the business owner does not need to purchase a new terminal to use the system. This form of mobile ordering and payment from MyOrder was a better fit with Rabobank's strategy. So, in August of 2012, they decided to buy out the IT company completely and acquire a large majority share in MyOrder.

Brinkman still owns 15 per cent of the shares in the company that grew out of his original idea. 'The road to market for an innovation such as MyOrder is predicated on creating a change in behaviour among consumers', he says:

That takes time and therefore also requires prolonged investment. At a certain point you realize that you cannot retain the majority of shares. If you want to grow, then you have to be able to let go of the idea of ownership and pursue the greater objective. You are better off having a smaller percentage of something successful than a large percentage of nothing.

Brinkman has found the partnership with Rabobank to be positive and fruitful:

> They are prepared to listen to the entrepreneur's side, as well, and not just look at their own interests as a bank. That was a big difference I noticed. The culture and mindset of someone who works at a large corporate organization, though, are of course very different from those of an entrepreneur who started from scratch. The value of money is really very different.

What MyOrder lacked was a large-scale market approach toward consumers. And Rabobank was the ideal candidate for providing that, in Brinkman's eyes:

> Rabobank could make MyOrder big. That's why I, as the concept's originator, was so enthusiastic about the deal, and I put in a lot of effort to help make that deal happen, influencing the other shareholders and massaging it along. Because that was what was going to determine our success.

When Rabobank took over MyOrder in 2012, it meant a huge transition for the venture's organization. The team doubled in size, going from 12 to 25 people; heavy investments were made on the sales and marketing side, in particular. At the same time, the very fact that a company like Rabobank was investing in the venture helped determine its rapid growth. As Brinkman says:

> That conveys an added level of certainty and confidence to business owners and consumers. We were working on a deal with Shell, and once we could announce that Rabobank was acquiring the business, it was an additional assurance for Shell, which made them think, 'We should go ahead and invest in this if Rabobank is going to back it'.

For Brinkman, the kick of entrepreneurship is still seeing his own product being used. He muses:

> You'll be sitting at a café on the beach or you'll go to the movies and you'll see people who are complete strangers all around you using the same app you thought up six years ago, see them going to the movies or ordering a drink with it. That's really cool. Or when you're driving down the motorway and you see billboards for MyOrder along the roadside: that's a huge rush. My ultimate dream is for it to become the standard method of payment in the Netherlands, the way debit cards are now.

People will eventually make payments with their mobile phones; the only question is when. Most of the development time has been devoted to a technology infrastructure for connecting businesses. Setting up that infrastructure for all those businesses takes a great deal of time and that is what Brinkman is investing heavily in at the moment. He concludes:

> So no matter what large player comes in – whether it's Google, PayPal or MasterCard – they are going to have to establish links to all those POS systems. And building those links takes a whole lot of work. That's a very good wall of protection for our idea and that is why we now have such a big head start. That was also the reason Rabobank didn't copy the idea but went ahead and bought it.

Four operational elements in the venture process

Use of a model

The venturing process at Rabobank is fairly new. At present it involves mostly a great deal of experimentation and learning. While the need for innovation is very real, there is little sense of urgency in terms of devoting resources to it. 'Changes in the bank landscape tend to occur very slowly', admits Dooijes:

> This is due in part to the fact that we are shielded by regulation, but also because banks have deep pockets and the impact of disruption is not immediately felt across the board. That disruption is occurring in the niches of our business and new entrants are nibbling away at pieces of the core banking business model.

One thing that is high on the agenda is scouting for innovative ideas. He continues:

> I ask the teams to share their insights with me; for instance, what is about to happen with a particular theme? And we also sponsor programmes by outside organizations, such as RockStart, Start-up Bootcamp and Village Capital. These are more cases of impact entrepreneurship but it is a conscious effort on our part to have that interaction with start-ups and be a part of things early on.

The amalgamated insights, contacts with start-ups and ideas are then translated into concrete plans and a strategy for putting those plans into practice using a Business Model Canvas (Figure 5.1). This does not adhere to the standard stage-gate model, however. Vollaard explains:

> We pose certain questions, but we do not work according to a business case. The very purpose of our innovation budget is to try things out: that is, test out concepts in real life to see if they are really worth pursuing and whether they really appeal to our customers. A good example is our recent introduction of mobile payments,

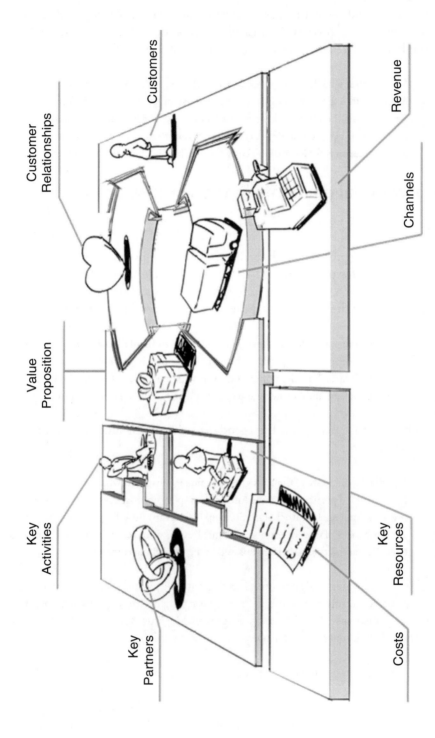

Figure 5.1 Business Model Canvas

like internet payments through your smartphone. We thought, 'That seems like it could be very useful'. Of course, there are all these online stores that want a mobile presence but they don't have any good method of payment. Well, why don't we try it out? So, we did. It was a big success and now we're rolling it out.

As soon as a venture is shown to have potential, it is pitched internally to secure the funding for putting it in motion. There is no set investment committee for this. Instead, pitches are made to the most relevant department or branch office, depending on the idea and target group. Vollaard admits:

That can be challenging, of course, because it's like do or die for each and every venture. And the more disruptive the innovation, the greater the challenge in making it happen. That is where the challenges exist, because you can't go to the Executive Board for funding every time you have an idea.

That means securing financial support from other departments, too, which is not always that easy. Particularly now that the financial industry is under such pressure, it never seems to be the right time for innovation. When things are going well, there is no need to invest because everything is fine. When things are not going well, and people recognize something should be done, it is difficult to get the money together and the focus is on the existing business. Moreover, support must be generated among the rank-and-file bank staff. On the other hand, one of the great advantages of a cooperative structure is the ability to shift gears quickly. Innovations developed with local banks can often be launched more successfully onto the market.

Portfolio

Vollaard's department primarily monitors trends to determine which ones might be of interest to Rabobank. These trends are discussed in so-called innovation sessions, during which the top ten are selected as potential innovation projects. Vollaard currently has some 30 innovation projects in his portfolio (Figure 5.2), with the goal being to shed about half of these every year ('kill your darlings'), so as to keep the level of innovation among projects high. 'Before you know it, the innovators can become a bit married to their project', says Vollaard.

Vollaard and his team focus primarily on ideas in the area of financial technology: big data, APIs (application programming interfaces), social media, mobile technology and the 'future of money' trend. Collaboration with a crowd-funding platform is part of that last trend. With Dooijes, he hopes to set up a FinTech fund for the bank that could be used in the future to invest in financial technology product innovations.

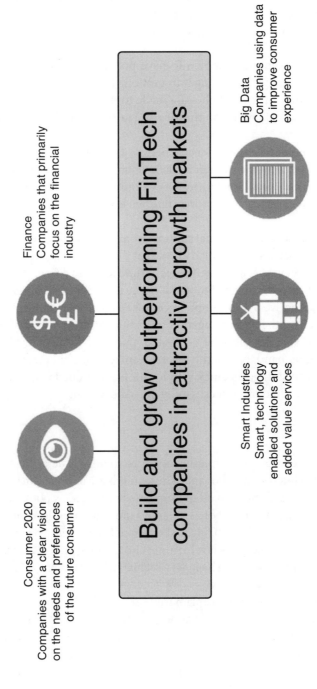

Figure 5.2 Portfolio of Rabobank's innovation and venturing projects

Consumer 2020
Companies with a clear vision on the needs and preferences of the future consumer

Finance
Companies that primarily focus on the financial industry

Build and grow outperforming FinTech companies in attractive growth markets

Big Data
Companies using data to improve consumer experience

Smart Industries
Smart, technology enabled solutions and added value services

Dooijes currently has two ventures up and running and a third in the works. The first is MyOrder, the mobile-commerce start-up in the smart technologies sphere that also verges on Consumer 2020 and big data, as discussed above. The second venture initiative is an e-invoicing platform. Investing in such a project is worthwhile for Rabobank because if it can become part of the purchasing transaction at an early stage in the process, that can become a bank transaction. Dooijes says:

> Imagine you are exporting a certain product X. That might eventually involve some exchange in which you need to interact with the bank – like getting financing or insurance – but that is relatively late in the process chain. If you can get in there earlier, then your relationship with that customer is much stronger and you are able to better help them. There is one earlier step – the purchase order – but even with invoicing, you are there from a very early stage. How can you help your customers in that supply chain? How can you optimize the financial supply chain management, as it were?

Another project Dooijes and his team focuses on is community banking. 'This is essentially a system that allows savings account holders at Rabobank to designate their savings for a particular purpose in a particular community', he explains. 'That is something we want to make very evident, so there's almost a one-to-one correspondence to what is actually being done with your money, with your access cash. That is another thing we are involved in, where we are now looking into how we are going to do that'. His team is constantly on the lookout for the next big thing, another example being disruptive trends in global remittances/P2P payments. Dooijes calls this 'Skype banking' and his team is currently analysing the impact on B2B international cash management and payments and working on formulating strategic advice for how to respond to this market development.

Team composition

Dooijes' team is a very mixed bunch. A few of his staff members form what he calls the academic conscience. 'They have strong analytical powers and can provide a quick and clear overview of things', he says. Then he has the entrepreneurial types, who like taking centre stage, who are enterprising and like building businesses. Finally, he will bring people on board with the requisite knowledge and expertise for a given project. 'The founding father of the mobile banking app for consumers is on my team', he says proudly.

He assembled his team 'by hand', by which he means that he personally picked the people. He says:

It's a fairly balanced composition, though limited in size. I started with four people and now I have a fifth, but lots of people want to join the team. I also have people on the periphery, who I cannot technically hire, because I don't have the budget for that, but who I tell, 'If you want to do this, you can go ahead'. They are the pockets of innovation we talked about. I try to motivate them and I involve them in the greater scheme.

His supervisor assigned him the task, in assembling his team, of bringing people in with think-tank capabilities. 'That means I need people who are interested in being open-minded and exploring new ideas, who can bring all that to the table. Those are the competencies I went looking for in people. They have to be people who aren't afraid to have their own opinions', he says.

Vollaard's team is similarly diverse: people who are good at communicating and networking, visionaries and deal-makers, the whole gamut. But there is a single common denominator among these multifarious professionals, as Vollaard points out:

Entrepreneurial spirit: the drive to seek change and not letting yourself be duped by whatever the core practice is. Your team also plays a vital part in that. Each person has their own projects and those almost always involve changes to the organization. So you always run into all sorts of obstacles, up against enormous resistance. Then it's nice if you can blow off steam collectively.

Relationship to the parent company

As mentioned earlier, the organization of innovation efforts at Rabobank is strongly influenced by the bank's cooperative structure. For the innovation projects Vollaard runs, the alignment between innovation and parent company is achieved by including an adopter, a sponsor and an architect for every project. These roles are filled by people from the parent organization who thus serve as the link between the innovation and its development in the standard business practices.

On Dooijes' team, the innovations they pursue are still primarily implemented from the bottom up. He points out:

I do always try to find supporters for our ideas who will think, 'Hey, what those guys are doing is cool'. That helps me. For instance, we held a conference where we invited 500 people from across the country. I was one of the speakers. It's something I actively pursue and it helps you create buy-in.

Another thing that helps create awareness and alignment between the pockets of innovation and the parent company is successful innovation, an excellent example of which is MyOrder.

New dynamic

Dooijes and his team have been handed some tough targets by management, primarily of a quantitative nature. In the MyOrder venture, for instance, they were judged according to the figures. Similarly, in the new business development arena, targets are numbers-based. 'I get evaluated on how many new business ideas have been presented, how many business ideas have been implemented, et cetera', Dooijes says.

Meanwhile, Dooijes has noticed that customer relations are also changing as a result of the venture initiative at Rabobank. 'It is no longer only the financial director or treasurer who maintains those relationships', he explains:

> We, for instance, sit down at the table with all these innovation managers from a wide range of companies who are Rabobank customers. And we come up with ideas there, too. We have now closed a deal with MyOrder and Shell. And that deal was concluded with a whole new group, which is to say the Marketing department at Shell. That has created an entirely new dynamic in customer relations, and we are an important part of that.

6

Eindhoven University of Technology's InnovationLab: commercializing scientific research for scientific research itself

Jessica van den Bosch and Geert Duysters

After receiving his degree in agricultural engineering from Wageningen University, Bart de Jong ended up doing IT work in the agricultural world. The technological expertise he acquired landed him a job a few years later with the Brabant Development Agency (BOM) in their Development & Innovation department. He worked there for 11 years and was charged with starter financing for the last six of those, during which he managed three funds for start-up companies. In mid-1999, the BOM Starters Center was given office space on the campus of Eindhoven University of Technology (TU/e). Within two years, De Jong was offered the director's position at Eutech Park, the university's incubator. That opportunity appealed to him, especially since he felt he had more to offer entrepreneurial companies than just helping them find funding. 'I thought the coaching aspect, helping people start their companies, was much more interesting', he says.

The birth of TU/e InnovationLab

At Eutech Park, De Jong initiated a grant proposal to establish the TU/e InnovationLab, which would specifically target innovation and commercialization at the university. Through a separate limited company set up specifically for that purpose, the grant money would be used to commercialize research, though no one really knew at that point how to do that. De Jong and his colleague Wim Bens decided to discuss the matter with a number of researchers at the university. Those talks convinced De Jong that the first priority had to be building awareness among the academic staff. He recalls:

> We decided that the first thing we had to do was try to convince our colleagues that the findings generated at a university should also carry over to business – and in a way that would actually be meaningful for business. We can come up with all the nifty new things we want at this university but that's not innovation. Innovation occurs when businesses combine technologies from a variety of disciplines, experiment with them and eventually create a product that can be sold on the market.

In the early days, De Jong and his partner Bens were primarily engaged in shepherding ideas through the first initial steps and supporting start-up companies. As De Jong says:

> We did not have any part in intellectual property (IP) issues, establishing IP rights or licensing them. That part was still dealt with in the General Affairs department. Everything was eventually integrated into a single group and it's all part of the TU/e InnovationLab now. That component is called Research Support, whereas my team and I are involved in business development [Figure 6.1].

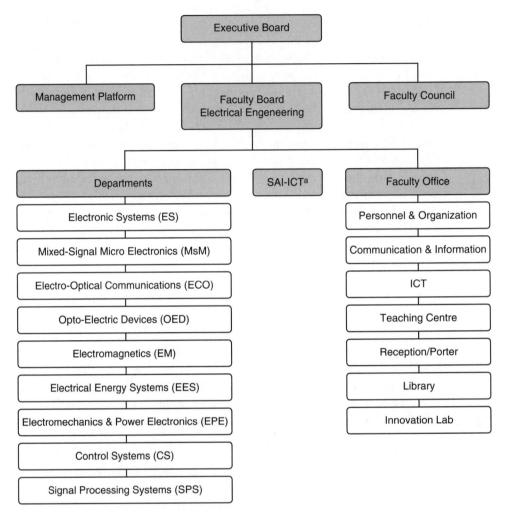

Note: a. SAI = Study Centre for Automatic Information Processing.

Figure 6.1 TU/e organogram

Today's TU/e InnovationLab can be denoted as the commercialization organization at Eindhoven University of Technology, home to research support, business development, the student incubator and a host of special university projects.

Spin-offs

His initial experiences made De Jong quickly realize that the university could do more with spin-offs. The distinction between start-ups and spin-offs is that the former refers to companies based on some generic knowledge possessed by the entrepreneur, such as a student or university employee. The idea, therefore, belongs to that person. In the case of spin-offs, the companies originate from some unique finding at the university (which may or may not have been patented yet). The thinking behind De Jong's focus in creating more spin-offs is that those (initially small) companies will grow into businesses the university can collaborate with at a later point in time, say in terms of research. 'The spin-offs emerging from this university tend to be companies that still need two to five years before they even get close to having a market-ready product. As a result, their attachment to the university is generally longer and more lasting than that of the start-ups', he says.

The TU/e InnovationLab learned a lot of valuable lessons from its first round of external funding. It has since secured follow-up funding through the commercialization scheme offered by Agentschap NL (NL Agency), a division of the Dutch Ministry of Economic Affairs that supports sustainable joint initiatives in developing entrepreneurship and innovation. This forced them to become more professional. 'One thing we learned, for example, was to be more explicit about why we were working on certain ideas and not others', De Jong points out:

> Another action we took was to appoint an investment committee made up of outside parties to whom we could present our plans. They could look at certain criteria and determine whether those were met. The process has become more transparent and professional, even internally. It used to be all based on a gut feeling. Entrepreneurship is, of course, and will always be, about gut feelings. It is not some mathematical calculation that you can hang your hat on and you never know if it will succeed: you are only able to make an estimation. But we have tried to turn that into best guesses.

A majority of the financing acquired is pre-seed funding that the start-ups and spin-offs can use to further develop their business idea into, for instance, a prototype. One of the ventures they supported is Synerscope.

Synerscope

From the business world to the research world . . . and back

Jan-Kees Buenen spent most of his career in the world of fast-moving consumer goods packaging in senior commercial roles. His talent for analytics and statistics quickly landed him a string of additional projects to build management information systems. Since the distribution chain for fast-moving consumer goods packaging is data-driven, competitiveness is based on information and information rates. 'The main goal was to be "better" in information services than the competitor', says Buenen:

> And that could be any kind of information, all the way from specific product-related order information to even supplying customers with marketing information, because as a packaging supplier, you have a much broader overview of things. I didn't just know things about one beer supplier; I knew things about every beer supplier in Europe. That's something you can use and then a huge data culture develops around you: big data.

The use of statistical process control to visualize machine output made it possible for that visual output to be interpreted by line operators. That insight led Buenen to a novel idea for knowledge worker departments: network visualization. The example he gives involves the visual depiction of behavioural patterns in, say, a certain department in an organization. He explains:

> In an office environment, you put people together in a certain structure and you expect a certain kind of behavioural interaction. You also try to manage that. Except, it would be helpful if you knew what the actual network of interactions and communications looked like. You could make that visible and you have to be able to scale it up to company size, meaning that you can make even more elements visible and that I can give it enough structure that I can teach you how to read that environment.

By visualizing such networks, you can discover patterns and find deviations. Those deviations can then be read, or interpreted, and the information used to make necessary adjustments in management. All of that helps you optimize behaviour in an organization. By detecting deviations in established trends at an early stage, managers can tackle and resolve unstable situations promptly.

The company

Buenen went looking for the technology to do just that. He found a lead in a scientific article written by Jac van Wijk, who in turn directed him to Danny Holten. At the time Holten was working on new technologies for visualizing network interactions, for his dissertation at TU/e. As it turned out, Holten was not only able to visualize large networks, but also include a time factor, making the views all that more meaningful: hierarchical edge bundling coupled with massive sequence views. Holten and Buenen joined forces in 2010 and, based on Holten's research and Buenen's vision emanating from his business experience, developed software that can make big data analyses 'readable' directly from log data without the need for end-users to have deep technical data querying skills. In 2011 they formalized their partnership by founding the company Synerscope.

The first thing they needed was a licence to operate and be able to claim future IP rights. Even though the idea was originally Buenen's, the technology had been developed by Holten as part of his doctoral research at TU/e. It was worthwhile for the TU/e InnovationLab to grant the licence to operate on behalf of the university because it might lead to a more extensive partnership in the future in that field of research, in perfect keeping with the lab's strategic objectives.

Once all of the legal matters had been settled and documented, they got down to business figuring out how Holten's technique could be adapted for manufacturing systems. They formed a team of PhD students and recent Master's graduates they knew from the Dutch university world. Buenen says:

> We chose people we knew. That is one of the most important aspects in a start-up: you want to bring in good staff. In our case, to build the product, we needed a team whose pedigree you are actually very familiar with. We brought together specialists from the fields of information visualization science with those from medical imaging. Then they started building.

Meanwhile, Buenen worked on the front end of the organization: fundraising and go-to-market strategy, and also started a bridgehead in the USA. 'Because we knew from the beginning that this was not merely a Dutch thing', he explains:

> We knew while we were developing and building it that it was intended for global enterprises. And we knew that to get it to really take off, we needed funding. So, it was a conscious decision from the outset. It is a unique technology; it is still going to require a great deal of research and we need to build markets. That means you need adequate funding. It would be a shame if you were to try to let it grow slowly, only to have someone with deeper pockets jump in. So, from the beginning we said, 'We need outside capital. We are not going to bootstrap this and then hope our first customer comes along; we are going in search of capital now'. This approach is similar to the way many Silicon Valley start-ups operate.

The first step for Synerscope in attracting outside capital was the traditional method used by most start-ups (i.e., after putting your own money in, you approach 'family, fools and friends'), but it was not long before they found seed investors. Buenen says:

Five Park Lane, one of our largest seed investors, which came on board in 2011, is made up of three former ABN-AMRO bank senior executives. They could see the potential applications of our software – not so much on the human resources side of things, but applications in the area of analysis and accounting, analysing financial flows. They knew of large potential clients from their former banking world.

In November 2011, Synerscope landed its first customer, in the USA: the National Insurance Crime Bureau. This was for the non-commercial version of the software, the so-called beta-plus version. 'We set out on two tracks', recalls Buenen:

> We knew it would take time to build a full commercial release. That was a project with a lead time from June 2011 to 30 March 2012 that five people would work on. But you can't wait that long before you try to sell the thing. So, Danny [Holten] said, based on his older work, 'You know what I'll do? I'll make a kind of intermediate version'. We called it 'beta plus'. Just like people always advise beginning entrepreneurs: make a minimal viable product and test it with customers as fast as you can. You have to dare to do that, put partially imperfect products on the market.

One of the most cited uses of big data is in fraud investigations. Buenen used that knowledge to convince a fraud expert to try the product in a demo. They tackled a dataset provided by the expert and what had taken the client six weeks with a team of two men to uncover took Buenen and his team just an hour. 'That drew us into the fraud business', he exclaims.

The trick was then keeping the sales pipeline full in an enterprise market with long sales cycles such as those of the financial industry, the primary focus at that time. 'You sometimes can get really lucky', says Buenen:

> If a financial institution is facing a critical fraud problem and has already allocated a budget for such things and is looking for a solution, then you can sell it in nine months. But if that is not the case, then the lead time can easily be as much as 12 months. Within months after the first customer, Delta Lloyd became our second.

The reason Synerscope is such a good fit for the insurance world is less its focus on combating fraud than the other possibilities the software offers: detecting disrupted patterns. 'Insurance data are extremely complicated', Buenen points out. 'Using traditional data analysis methods on them is highly time-consuming, making it tremendously expensive for the insurers. So it simplifies things if someone shows up with a tool where you load your raw data and they can already start identifying things three hours later'.

This might not necessarily be related to fraud; more often the discoveries involve process changes. In the end, these yield very useful information for an organization because they provide insight into where processes need to be improved. Buenen is now working on expanding his scope beyond the financial world, as well. One promising area is operations research for the purchasing processes of large, complex organizations.

There are three separate aspects to the relationship between Synerscope and the TU/e InnovationLab. In addition to the licence to operate for the software that they received from the university and the office space they rent on campus, they are participating in research in the form of funding a doctoral project. These interactions meld seamlessly with the strategic objectives pursued by the TU/e InnovationLab: to create an ecosystem/network of companies with which to work together on the research front.

Buenen and his business partner have a big ambition: to build a large, healthy, global company. At the same time, Buenen realizes that things can easily pan out differently for software companies:

> If, midway through, some company comes along and says 'I can do something better with that', then we'll see. That's one of the main points of being an entrepreneur: you have to be prepared to take advantage of opportunities when they come up and, if any problems arise, to get to work resolving them.

Four operational elements in the venture process

So how does the TU/e InnovationLab make use of a model? Do they have a portfolio of ventures they wish to support? Is team composition of any relevance to them? And how is the relationship between the ventures and the parent company structured, if at all?

The stage-gate model at the TU/e InnovationLab

The business developers at the TU/e InnovationLab cycle proactively through the university's departments on the lookout for interesting new activities. 'We talk to the researchers; we look at the kinds of projects being performed; and we try to unearth the kinds of things that might be of interest to business or could be used for setting up a spin-off', explains De Jong. That process generates 150–200 leads a year.

As soon as they discover an idea that seems valuable, they ask the researcher to fill in an invention disclosure form. To prove grounds for the patent, they need the researcher's input, especially for communicating with the patent authorities. Those bodies will pose questions about the idea that only the researcher is in a position to answer clearly. Accordingly, the researchers remain closely involved in the process.

The invention disclosure form offers business developers their initial foothold for pursuing an idea. The form lists the inventors and the invention itself, but also any competing inventions. De Jong explains:

> We ask researchers what they think the market is, which companies might be interested. That is our initial basis for proceeding and the more we know from their perspective, the less we have to discover ourselves because they already knew all that. It's knowledge that's ready to go. That is our starting point. But we're not filing for patents for the sake of it. Only when we have a gut feeling that this could lead to a positive business case do we put in the effort necessary for obtaining a patent.

If the idea is eligible for a patent claim, then the invention disclosure form is sent to the intellectual property officer, who examines it to make sure it contains everything necessary and determines whether the idea is patentable. This also involves looking into how the research is being funded, which is an important factor in determining the freedom to operate. If the research is being funded by another institution, then that organization can claim all the property rights and the TU/e InnovationLab will not be involved in the commercialization process, or only to a limited extent.

The process from idea inception to completing the quick scan (is it viable and worth the effort?) generally takes about four months. As soon as an idea is found worthy for the TU/e InnovationLab to start working on, it is time to write the business case. This process also generally lasts about four months, with an additional two months for dotting the i's and crossing the t's. Once the case has been finished and presented, a decision needs to be made about whether to proceed with the idea. That decision is taken jointly by the business developers, whereupon the case is submitted to a panel of experts. This is an ad hoc panel of outside parties brought in to brainstorm about who and what is needed to make the business case even stronger. De Jong admits:

> It's tough on our pride when a case is rejected, and sometimes we might have completely overlooked things that the expert panel uncovers that make the entire business case non-viable. When that happens, it's a shame, but we would rather have it happen at that point than after we have established the business. Rejection is very rare, however, probably because we are so discerning ourselves. We sometimes ask ourselves if we aren't *too* discerning. Especially when you realize

that between 80 per cent and 90 per cent of our spin-offs still exist, whereas the national average is 50 per cent. On the one hand, I think perhaps we should be somewhat less discerning; on the other, maybe we ended up sparing a great many people a great deal of misery. That is the trade-off you have to weigh in your mind every time.

The input from the expert panels is used to hone the case and make it more solid. After ten months, the case is finished, and if a patent is involved, that is definitely a critical deadline. After a year, the Patent Cooperation Treaty (PCT) procedure has to be started. PCT prolongs the patent, allowing you to retain your rights worldwide. However, it costs between €12 000 and €15 000, so it is not something to be taken lightly, especially since there is no guarantee of success.

The business case is used as a basis for determining what the best business model is: licensing the invention to existing businesses or developing a spin-off. Under the first scenario, the developers approach parties with whom to enter into licensing agreements. In situations where the case seems better suited to creating a spin-off, a business incubation officer is appointed, who will slowly but surely take over the reins from the business developer. De Jong says:

> If we believe we have a very strong business idea, but it is not yet something we can sell to businesses, we will set up a company ourselves. That starts in the form of a wholly-owned subsidiary of this university, for which we usually seek an outside person to assume the role of Chief Executive Officer. If the researcher wants to remain involved, then he or she becomes the Chief Technology Officer.

With the legal entity established (limited company), the next step is to decide how much investment is needed and where to get it. The Business Incubation Officer works together with the CEO to approach various companies and refine the business plans and get them ready to show investors. Funding might take the form of a pre-seed loan or it might be a proof-of-concept loan. The first kind of financing supports the spin-off in launching the business; the second is generally an investment to be used for working the idea up into a prototype.

The Business Incubation Officer remains on board through the initial venture round. Once an external party shows interest – someone who is not just a business angel, but more of a venture capitalist – then the TU/e InnovationLab's involvement is nearing its end. De Jong explains:

Investors tend to demand so much in the shareholders' agreement that they assume a very real role in the process. It isn't long before the venture capitalist appoints a CFO, for example: 'We want control of the finances'. Then our job is done, because after all, the Business Incubation Officer can obviously only oversee so many companies.

As a party in the holding company, TU/e's only role at that point is as a shareholder and it actually aspires to an early exit. De Jong concludes:

The added value of spin-offs and licences is not the royalty we receive, not that dividend and not the exit. Even a place like MIT, no slouch in that regard, only receives about 8–10 per cent of its research budget from those sorts of things – a drop in the ocean. The true added value lies in creating an ecosystem around this university by attracting, through the spin-offs, R&D groups that want to locate near the university, work with it to perform research and bring in the funding needed for that.

The strategic objective of the TU/e InnovationLab is thus to attract money for research and not to sell knowledge. With that in mind, knowledge is sometimes 'deposited' with businesses in exchange for a research contract or a project that will generate new intellectual property. It's called the 'Easy Access Model'. This helps link businesses to the university and create a knowledge ecosystem.

Portfolio

Based on insights from the business world that the intersection of various technologies could lead to products with commercial value, TU/e decided about three years ago to designate three specific strategic areas: health, energy and smart mobility. These themes transcend university department boundaries, thereby requiring multidisciplinary engagement by their very nature. De Jong stresses:

They cut right through all of the departments, and what you find is that at the intersections where departments overlap, that's where the best things originate – not through monoculture, but an industrial designer working with someone from electrical engineering or someone from electrical engineering working with a chemist. Time and again, that's where the greatest ideas originate.

Nevertheless, De Jong does not use these three themes as a guiding precept in determining whether or not certain ventures can be launched as part of some portfolio. Their existence does underscore the thinking that multidisciplinary research produces interesting innovation possibilities, so the three new business developers at the TU/e InnovationLab are each connected to a particular theme, in addition to being in charge of certain departments. The three strategic areas are used, therefore, in the screening and scouting process.

Team composition

The TU/e InnovationLab has over 30 employees in total. Most of them are involved in research support. De Jong's team consists of six people who focus almost entirely on the venturing aspects. Over the past few years, the brunt of the activities has shifted from supporting beginning companies to business development. And by that, De Jong means that his team has gone looking for more opportunities for transferring knowledge from the university to business. De Jong explains:

> We have become much more proactive instead of reactive in our activities. We now go into the university to find out what's happening, where we might be able to help. In the beginning, we just sat here, and if something happened to come our way, then we snapped it up. Now, even if I had ten business developers, I could keep all ten of them busy. The way we have it organized now means that we are also forced to make choices. At some point we just have to say 'No, this won't work' or 'Yes, that's it'. We go in proactively; we search for things; we try to get as many leads as possible . . . but then we have to draw a very definite line: this is interesting and this isn't. Our job at that point is to tell the researcher why we don't think it's interesting. It's not a denunciation of his research, because that's not what it's about. We look at it from the viewpoint of: do we think anyone is waiting around for this knowledge and might even be prepared to take a risk on it?

Originally, the staff were made up primarily of people who had a sound technological understanding of the discipline they were assigned to provide support for. As the working methodology became more oriented to business development, the competencies required also changed, with more emphasis on entrepreneurial skills, creativity and business administration. But in a technological environment, you also need people who understand that the research a scientist is working on is often like his 'child'. 'Then you reach a point where you need people capable of understanding that you can't simply snatch away that research', says De Jong. 'You have to be tactful and aware of the sensitivities, to coax that researcher a few steps forward to the point where he is able to say, "I think it's a good idea for you to take this over now and I will continue on with my research"'.

Association between a venture and the TU/e InnovationLab

It is not part of the TU/e InnovationLab's strategic objective to integrate start-ups into its own business processes; in fact, it is practically the reverse. By positioning itself as a partnering agent creating and supporting ventures, they aim to build a lasting relationship with these ventures and external partners in order to create something much more important for the university's future: research funding.

An added benefit of building such partnerships with start-ups is that it helps bring in funding for research projects from grant proposals. One trend in that area is a preference for consortia made up of research institutions working with small and medium enterprises (SMEs). 'We are thus creating our own network of partners', De Jong points out:

> Especially when it comes to the new European grant projects, SMEs are very important. We create our own SMEs right here, so we have our pick of them. The more parties we manage to gather around this university – and by that I mean not just physically, but ones with ties to our university – the easier it is to form consortia.

The future of the TU/e InnovationLab

In the past, the TU/e InnovationLab was fortunate enough to receive various grants and other project funding that it used to set up the organization and achieve its initial successes. De Jong currently relies on revolving funds and proof-of-concept loans. The basic concept is that if a start-up receives funding under such a financial structure and then achieves success, a certain sum of money will be paid back into the fund for investing in new projects. 'Our experience has been that about 60–65 per cent gets paid back. Since we used to be relatively flexible in granting the funding, we expect that under the current structure, we will probably have a fund that truly is revolving within about six years', says De Jong.

Besides securing a financial foundation for continuity, having an enthusiastic, motivated team is an absolute prerequisite to remaining successful in the venturing business, according to De Jong. 'No one here has that nine to five mentality, and as far as I know everybody looks forward to coming to work every day', he says. 'We all have a certain level of experience and you try to share that experience with others. That is not to say that they have to do what I say. The point is, "Learn from what I already know"'.

7

SanomaVentures: innovating by attracting entrepreneurial talent

Arjan van den Born and Jessica van den Bosch

Sanoma started in 1913 as a Finnish company that published magazines (Sanoma means 'message' in Finnish). The Dutch company, Sanoma Media, was created in 2001, when the Sanoma Group acquired the magazine division of the Dutch publishing company VNU, along with its subsidiary 'ilse media'. It has a market position in every segment of the media industry: popular magazines, television broadcasting, events, consumer media, e-commerce, sites and apps. Sanoma Group is a media and learning company that provides information and entertainment across many European countries.

Sanoma Media has pursued a takeover campaign in recent years, including acquiring SBS Broadcasting Group in 2011. Taking over companies was becoming expensive, however, yet Sanoma still wanted to continue investing in growth and innovation. This produced a need for finding creative ways of doing that.

Innovation at Sanoma

Sanoma established two initiatives within the company, whose focus was to stimulate innovation and entrepreneurship. The company's Future Media Team works with internal ventures. It has designed a rigorous programme that encourages staff members to come up with new business ideas and bring them to Sanoma. The ideas are pitted against one another in a competition format and the winning concepts are developed further. The point is to promote entrepreneurship among Sanoma employees.

SanomaVentures, meanwhile, focuses on outside venture opportunities in the hope of catalysing innovation in the media industry, targeting, in particular, initiatives in the area of digital information, entertainment and learning resources. By actively shepherding promising start-ups as they enter their initial stage of growth, SanomaVentures aims to help those businesses achieve that growth. It does this by offering them operating capital, sharing knowledge and providing them with access to the media industry network. The start-ups also receive support in the form of financial and strategic coaching.

SanomaVentures is led by investment directors Herman Kienhuis and Antoine Hendrikx. Kienhuis originally trained as a chemical engineer but after completing his education he quickly became interested in strategic consultancy. He first made a career at McKinsey, before joining Sanoma as a strategist in 2004, where he also gained experience in acquisitions and leading digital product development at ilse media. Hendrikx studied business administration at Tilburg University and then landed a job with Ernst & Young, where he held various positions in the Netherlands and England.

He joined Sanoma as a controller and two years later became the CFO of ilse media/Sanoma Digital. Kienhuis started SanomaVentures in 2012 and Hendrikx joined six months later.

Strategic goals

From SanomaVentures' viewpoint there are three strategic reasons for investing in interesting start-ups. The first is that they noticed an increasing tendency among young talent to opt for entrepreneurship instead of a corporate career. Moreover, in the world of digital media, that step toward independent entrepreneurship is relatively easy to take: not much is required to start and there is tremendous flexibility. 'We think it is vital for us to align ourselves with talented entrepreneurs, so we do that in this way, by investing in them', says Kienhuis.

The second compelling reason is the need for creating strategic options as pathways to growth. With the future being so difficult to predict, even in the short term, it is essential to bet on more than one horse. 'You do that by investing in a sufficient number of start-ups', Kienhuis continues. 'We obviously also maintain a clear overview of it all, because the growth has to be in line with what the parent company Sanoma envisions'.

The third, and final, reason is the power that SanomaVentures has to create added value. It does this by not only investing money, but also, perhaps more so, by deploying its media outlets to give the start-ups quicker access to customers, so that they can achieve accelerated growth and add a wide range of expertise from Sanoma's own online businesses, as VirtuaGym did.

VirtuaGym: a Sanoma venture

In early 2008, Hugo Braam and his brother Paul quit their jobs to concentrate full-time on starting their own business. The brothers had been bitten by the entrepreneurship bug early in life; when they were young, they used to program their own games together, a development that continued into their college days. 'We always kind of felt like, "Wow, dude, it'd be cool if we could make things together". I'm always getting lots of ideas that I send on to my brother. I guess I'm the creative link. My brother is more of the down-to-earth type', recalls Hugo Braam. Their idea was to develop a new technology to assist people in living a healthier, more active life – a kind of sensor device that measures your movements and you can use to exercise at home. 'We came up with a good technology for doing that and we patented it, quit our jobs and got started', he continues.

In the first six months, they developed a prototype and managed to get an investor interested in their product. The business plan had been drawn up and the manufacturing and logistics thought out, when they got wind of an Israeli company that was developing a 3D camera that could detect movement. 'That company became Kinect, the technology Microsoft launched on such a big scale', says Braam. 'At the time, I think it was a good decision for us to kill our product but then you're left thinking, after putting those six months in, "What now?"' The two brothers eventually decided to focus on solely creating the platform and software behind it. 'That platform became VirtuaGym', Braam continues, 'and we're now running the system around the world, with delivery to more than three million consumers'.

After terminating their first product, it took them just under a year to develop the software product, whereupon they won backing from an incubator and found their first investor, who was willing to provide seed funding. 'Of course, we still had relevant know-how and insight into the market and needs, so it's not like all of the effort from that first product development had been wasted', Braam points out. The business incubator not only put them in contact with their first investor, but also provided suitable workspace. 'That allowed us to hire interns and make a lot of headway quickly in developing the idea', he adds.

VirtuaGym provides people with support from a self-management perspective. 'We try to help them achieve lasting lifestyle change through personalized training and nutrition programmes, which we offer within a community using the freemium model', explains Braam. What that means, in practice, is that users can download a basic version of the programme for free but must pay separately to obtain customized measurements. Current versions of the platform can also be customized for commercial clients according to the needs of their staff or customers, including being branded with the organization's own corporate identity and logo. This could appeal to fitness centres, personal trainers, health care organizations and other such businesses. What makes the product unique is the totality of the system. 'There is almost no other programme that offers such a rich consumer experience in terms of solutions, especially in combination with tools for coaching people', he says.

The seed funding they received to make their initial foray brought them into contact with Kienhuis at SanomaVentures. That initial contact eventually resulted in a more extensive collaboration, which evolved into the company's venture investment in VirtuaGym in early 2013. Sanoma has a number of strong brands in the media industry that constitute an enticing target group for VirtuaGym. The appeal lies not so much in the media support Sanoma can offer through the advertising it provides, but much more in the fact that Sanoma is a strong online player and knows a great deal about digital development and online marketing. In addition, partnerships with Sanoma magazines such as *Margriet* or *Libelle* provide opportunities for establishing brand portals. Braam says with a laugh:

> And we have found, since we teamed up with SanomaVentures, that it forces us to be more professional in managing our start-up: periodic follow-ups, financial reports . . . It has forced us to change from pretty much a club with a group of nerds who think it's fun to roll out a product to really being a more sales target-driven organization.

In exchange for its investment in VirtuaGym, SanomaVentures received a minority interest in the start-up. That means that the two brothers still lead the company in terms of the strategic direction they want to take, though they also take full advantage of the expertise and experience that Kienhuis and Hendrikx can provide in terms of expanding the company. Braam continues:

> We consider it a tremendous advantage to have a mirror like that: people who are committed to our company but who come from the outside and therefore bring a totally different perspective to the business and have other ideas. It forces us to think about why we look at certain things in a particular way and what we want to achieve with that.

In the last five years, VirtuaGym has gone from being a two-person start-up to a company that employs 12 people. In those five years, they have also worked with a lot of interns. 'At the time, that was a very good way for us to be lean but still have a lot of help and be able to quickly prototype things as a basis for further developing the product. In all, we've had something like 50 interns over the past five years', says Braam. Another big advantage of this is that they now have a network of people they know well, including their capabilities, who they can turn to for specific assignments or projects. Braam is drawn, in particular, to proactive types who provide constructive input. 'We don't pretend to know everything ourselves. So, if someone has more specialized knowledge in their field of expertise than we do, then it's quite possible that he has a better idea about how, exactly, we should tackle something in that field', he says.

Now the company is focused on international growth. In mid-2013, they landed the largest fitness chain in New Zealand as a client. 'That was a huge milestone for us', Braam says. 'The customer commissioned extensive market research from three separate agencies and all three of them indicated that we were the best company to join forces with – to the detriment of our American competitor. That's when you know you have a competitive product'.

Before that many of their international sales were to personal trainers in Australia and America. Because their product is internationally accessible, they don't need to set up branch offices to get it operational in other markets. Braam says:

> But for a large market like America, you do have to promote it by advertising in fitness magazines, because it's worthless to only sell to that market through online forums. So, we are actively looking into whether we should either find a partner to seriously gain some traction in America or set something up there ourselves.

Reflecting back on the past five years, Braam admits that if he and his brother had it to do all over again, they would approach things differently. 'We would do something much smaller', he says, 'that you could get onto the market much more quickly: find a customer immediately and, based on that, start earning money right away, then develop the product further'. For the time being, they have their hands full realizing their international ambitions.

Four operational elements in the venture process

Stage-gate model

Last year, SanomaVentures invested in eight start-up companies. It uses the traditional stage-gate model in doing so. Of course, since they are investing in businesses that have already been started, the first and second stages (idea generation and business plan development) do not apply in their case.

It all starts with an intake discussion with the start-up. If this leaves a positive impression on the venture team, it will be followed by a formal pitch. Hendrikx explains:

> The pitches are held for a few members of our board and some business owners, generally a group of about eight people. Our CFO and legal expert are also present. They have an hour to pitch their idea. It's partly about the product, but also about the people. In fact, we tell them, 'Bring your management team'. We are, after all, investing in people.

If the pitch is positively received, then a term sheet will be drafted in the next few weeks. This lays out the terms and conditions and main agreements of the proposed relationship and forms the basis for the eventual decision document the board will use in its final go/no-go evaluation. 'Any go decisions are naturally followed by due diligence before the contract is finalized and signed', Hendrikx adds (see Figure 7.1).

3 wks	3 wks	3 wks	3 wks	3 wks
1. Orientation	2. Assessment	3. Planning & Negotiation	4. Decision-Making	5. Execution
• Business plan screening • Meet the team • Info document	• Pitch to group • Investment assessment • 1st round feedback from experts • Term sheet	• Discuss roadmap budget and mediaplan • Investment and option agreement	• 2nd round feedback from experts • Investment proposal	• Due diligence investigation • DD report • Finalize and sign contracts • Media sales

Figure 7.1 The investment process

Despite SanomaVentures' relatively late entry into the process, assembling a good selection out of all the interesting start-ups out there remains an intense, time-consuming exercise. In that sense, their selection process is no less extensive than what generally happens during the first stage of innovation when searching for potentially suitable ideas. 'Out of 150 business plans we receive, maybe five will receive an investment', Kienhuis points out:

> You waste a whole lot of time on things that aren't going anywhere, so you have to be as efficient as possible. The use of standard documentation and a standard process can help. We've noticed that, certainly with the successful start-ups and the ones with a lot of promise, they have several irons in the fire, several potential investors in mind. So if you can be transparent and say, 'This is the process; this is what we're going to do; this is the documentation . . . , then it helps increase your chances of winning over the start-up.

As mentioned, SanomaVentures invested in eight start-ups last year. Given the overall objective of signing up 20 start-ups within a total period of three years' time for investing and three years' time for managing, that is not a bad outcome for their first year. The total investment they have to allocate is approximately €10 million, consisting not only of hard cash, but also media support. 'You need money for any good plan; that's pretty much the thinking', says Hendrikx. 'We have the wind at our backs right now. It's clear to everyone that print is a tough market, so this company is actively looking for new streams of revenue'.

That target of 20 start-ups is not set in stone. The parent company management feels that quality is more important than quantity. The remaining five years will be used primarily therefore for learning and gaining experience. 'We already, after just our first year, have so many issues to think about', says Hendrikx:

> How are we going to scale it up? Should we, for instance, ramp up to 100 ventures or should we expand to Germany or other countries? It is definitely taking off, but we have to wait and see how strong their stomachs still are when a couple start failing down the line, because it's bound to happen sometime. There is, in principle, a board document outlining an investment period of three years. And we clearly stated ahead of time, 'If you are looking for some quick revenue, this is not it. This really requires some lead time'. It'll take several years before you really get a good idea of what is happening.

The initial investment in the start-ups takes the form of a convertible loan. While that may sound fairly risk-free, the fact is that, even then, if the business runs into trouble the investment is lost. Only after that initial step, do they move on to possible shareholding. This tactic was chosen as the best option, mostly because it makes the process a lot simpler. To some extent it's also because of the early stage at which many of the ventures are. 'Some start-ups might not have yet, or not properly, handled certain matters, such as security or privacy. Before you know it, you see a headline that reads, "Sanoma site hacked . . ." All eyes are on the big guys; it's something we have to be careful about', explains Hendrikx.

The premise is that the ventures should grow to millions in revenues in three years. As long as SanomaVentures is a minority shareholder, it will receive nothing more than dividends. But that is not the aim. The real deliverable is the strategic value of the venture: in other words, creating future revenue streams and not necessarily short-term profits. 'Start-ups are absolutely not supposed to pay out dividends the first ten years', stresses Hendrikx. 'We actually hope that it will be re-invested in that start-up, so that the start-up grows more quickly'.

Portfolio

SanomaVentures has designated six areas it wants to be active in:

- online consumer services;
- mobile and tablet applications;
- online video and connected TV;
- online advertising and marketing;
- e-learning and personal development;
- e-commerce.

One additional, important criterion is that SanomaVentures only invests in companies with a live product and a few early adopter customers. They purposely do not invest in ideas or plans. In part, this is from the perspective that doing so would open them up to far too much uncertainty, but there is also the fact that the kind of value SanomaVentures can add becomes most relevant when the business is up and running. 'We feel that, at this point, we can add the most value at that particular stage, because that's when those media truly start to become interesting and that's when our know-how is worthwhile in terms of improving things', Kienhuis points out. 'What's more, Sanoma also invests in product development on its own. The focus for Ventures, then, is on investing in the start-ups that Sanoma does not have the time or resources for, developments that would otherwise not get off the ground'.

The six areas listed above are broadly defined and meld seamlessly with the parent company's strategic areas. In terms of strategic investment, the ultimate goal for the long term is to integrate all of the businesses into the parent company. Hendrikx says:

> We do not put this down in writing, and if it turns out it would be better to disinvest or a better investor comes along, we are prepared to do that, but in principle everything is geared toward combining the new businesses with us later on. That might only happen in half the cases, but that is the fundamental premise; we are very clear about that.

Relationship to parent company

Sanoma is a company that operates internationally. Yet, Kienhuis's Ventures organization has a local orientation with regard to scouting for start-ups. The main reason for this is that investors like to be close to the start-ups, so that the lines of communication are short. The focus for the start-ups themselves is nevertheless international, because the Dutch market is too small for most digital businesses.

The initial idea behind the venture initiatives is to have a means of integrating relevant developments into the parent company in the future. That future integration is taken into consideration from the moment the pitch is given, by bringing in a business owner who has an affiliation with the parent company. He or she contributes valuable expertise and is included in many of the meetings with the start-up. As Hendrikx explains:

> That way, you create this link that benefits everyone and builds familiarity. In some specific cases, we include an option, if the venture agrees, for taking it to 51

per cent, in which case we explain in advance how we plan to do that and where it would end up.

The intention, therefore, is to increase Sanoma's interest in the start-ups and obtain a majority percentage. But since the investments are being made at a relatively early point in the process, it is difficult to predict, going in, whether or not that can or will happen. 'We are pragmatic in that regard', Kienhuis adds:

> Look, anything can happen along the way. If someone comes along who would like to purchase it for a good price . . . , then, sure, that could be an option. So it is also about seeing what happens, and we don't want to project too far forward either, because there's not much point. And we believe in the independence of the entrepreneur.

Team composition

When assessing start-ups to invest in Kienhuis and Hendrikx look at things like market activity and scalability. Kienhuis explains:

> One of our golden rules is that the company has to possess the technology. If you want to move quickly, then you need that in your team; so we consider their IT person to be an important factor. Another important element, in addition to the self-reliability you might expect of an entrepreneur, is the entrepreneur's flexibility, given that the plan might have to be adapted at any point depending on the circumstances.

A decision has already been taken for one of the ventures not to pursue it further. It turned out that Sanoma was not the right partner. The entrepreneur looked for another partner and found one, who took over the investment at a reasonable price. There are also some doubts about a couple of the other ventures. 'One of the ventures, for instance, needed a new infusion of capital and we had some misgivings', says Hendrikx. 'In the end, we said, "Sorry, we aren't giving you another euro; we'll just have to cut our losses". Then they got a new burst of energy all of a sudden and it took off again. Bootstrapping does force people to be creative'.

The future

SanomaVentures was structured as a project. It will receive investment funding for three years to build the portfolio. Kienhuis and Hendrikx will then be given another three years to manage that portfolio. 'The entire plan has a six-year horizon, but that is how I proposed it, and along the way it's entirely possible that we continue investing, so that it runs a bit longer', says Kienhuis.

The project's success is determined in terms of not only the financial targets it attains, but also, for instance, the amount of PR generated, the expertise and experience they acquire and the growth opportunities they manage to create. 'The sales growth for the companies we've invested in, that is also an important objective, since if Sanoma wants to boost turnover, having majority interests and being able to consolidate are attractive options. That adds turnover to your own company, too', Hendrikx explains.

The planning from the outset is not to create a revolving fund. A six-year term is not conducive to that; it is too short to start generating any meaningful profit on the investment. That should, of course, start happening after those six years. At the moment, efforts are more focused on achieving growth for the ventures and consolidating that turnover growth.

There is, as always, room for improvement, though this amounts primarily to the finer details of reporting. 'It's true that everything could be tighter. Many of the reports to the board, for example, which makes up the investment committee, are still done by hand and that should definitely be more automated. Those kinds of things could be better', admits Hendrikx.

SanomaVentures is currently in the process of creating an international network to further assist the start-ups with international potential. 'The big advantage we have is our international renown through the parent company', says Hendrikx:

> We can gain access to places the start-ups would never get into. For the moment we are mostly doing that in countries where we already have a presence, such as Finland and Russia. Sanoma's footprint, however, is not typically in the countries start-ups want to be in. They tend to lean more toward places like the UK, the USA, Germany, France, et cetera. We are trying to expand that by actively engaging in internationalization.

The partnerships to date have primarily resulted from sales deals, but in an effort to start partnerships with, for instance, venture capitalists, more thought will be given to their structure and who can bring what to the table.

The venturing world is relatively small. Many of the venture organizations meet up at boot camps and other networking opportunities. Nevertheless, SanomaVentures is a partner that sets itself apart. As Hendrikx says:

We have created good press by giving positive feedback to the ventures that approach us about possible partnerships, even those we don't end up doing business with. And if we know someone who might be a better fit for them as a partner, we'll give them that reference. Silicon Valley became what it is by sharing things and not being afraid to share. You see that happening now in the venturing world and you don't see it in the old European economy much. I think that was one of the reasons for their success and we try to live by that.

8

nrc·next: reinventing printed news*

Jessica van den Bosch and Victor Gilsing

Folkert Jensma discovered his love of journalism as a student at Leiden University when he started writing for the university weekly, *Mare*. Then, as a newly graduated lawyer, he started working freelance for the Science section of the Dutch newspaper *NRC Handelsblad*. By staying put when his contract as a temp ran out, he more or less forced his bosses to accept him as a regular staff member at the newspaper. 'Squatting the masthead', he calls it, enjoying the fact that under Dutch law, keeping on temporary staff can automatically result in a permanent contract. After passing through various editorial teams, he became editor-in-chief when his predecessor, Ben Knapen, unexpectedly accepted a position on the board of Philips Electronics. Knapen's deputy at the time decided not to take over the role, so Jensma, a relative junior at 38 and an outsider, was the surprise choice.

By the late 1990s, newspapers around the world were confronting a sea change in media behaviour, partly as a result of the increasing possibilities afforded by the internet. NRC decided to study these changes and the resulting market analysis boiled down to this: the market was highly competitive. More subscribers were being lost than new ones signed up, due to the ever-growing surge in free news sources – from free newspapers and online and broadcast news sites to digital media – which, moreover, were available 24 hours a day, seven days a week. Among the younger demographic in particular, there was a distinct drop in interest and subscriptions, putting the traditional earnings model under pressure. The fact is, subscriptions generate the most stable income. In a booming economy, advertising has been known to generate 70 per cent of a publisher's income, whereas when the economy is failing that percentage can drop to 30 per cent. Subscriptions generally are less susceptible to the economic cycle.

NRC Handelsblad and PCM Uitgevers

NRC Handelsblad is a daily evening quality newspaper published in the Netherlands, currently by NRC Media. The newspaper was launched on 1 October 1970 as the result of a merger between *Algemeen Handelsblad* (est. 1828) and *Nieuwe Rotterdamsche Courant* (est. 1844). Until 2009, *NRC Handelsblad* was part of the publishing group PCM Uitgevers (Figure 8.1), which also published the Dutch newspapers *De Volkskrant*, *Trouw* and *Algemeen Dagblad*. Each of these dailies operated independently within PCM, with the four newspapers actually being competitors of one another.

PCM Uitgevers assigned Jensma, as editor-in-chief of *NRC Handelsblad*, the task of either acquiring a bigger market share within that deteriorating market or strengthening *NRC Handelsblad*'s position by capturing a share of some new market. It is not so much that the total time consumers devote to media has decreased in the past couple decades, as that newspapers as a medium account for a smaller portion of that. TV, radio and internet have all grown in terms of consumption time.

'In the world of newspapers, you only have a limited number of options for winning back the attention of the newspaper-reading public', Jensma explains. 'The first is to change the time of day you publish. Almost all of the evening papers around the world have switched to morning delivery'. That saves money because the production process is easier; a morning paper does not have to be printed at three different locations in the country and then distributed during the afternoon rush hour. 'But beyond that', Jensma adds, 'it gives the paper a longer use life: morning papers provide people a longer

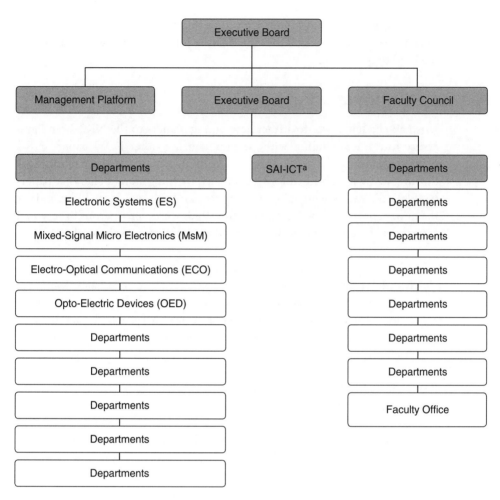

Note: a. SAI = Study Centre for Automatic Information Processing.

Figure 8.1 PCM organogram

reading time: the entire day'. The other three newspapers in the PCM Group, which were all morning papers, were obviously opposed to the notion of *NRC Handelsblad* switching from an evening newspaper to a morning one, which meant that option was ruled out from the beginning.

A second option is to change the format, for example from a broadsheet to a tabloid size. In the case of *NRC Handelsblad*, transitioning to a tabloid format was not an option because all of the newspapers published by PCM Uitgevers were printed and distributed together, so they all had to be the same size. That meant that idea was no solution, either. The final option is adjusting the price, but the premium price the quality *NRC Handelsblad* could charge had always been seen as its biggest asset. So the innovation would have to come from either the existing product or a new one. That was the bind they were in.

A need to innovate: but how?

Jensma's challenge was to attract new, young readers to the NRC brand and assure future exploitation without cannibalizing other PCM papers. *NRC Handelsblad* started by focusing on creating a digital news environment through its own website, informed, in part, by the general belief that paper-based media really were going to disappear and this would spell the end for the newspaper industry. In addition, the 1990s were a prosperous time, when a great deal was possible from a financial perspective. Jensma recalls:

> Riding that wave, we were wondering, 'How are we going to accommodate all this, while retaining our operating basis?' So we put a lot of time, money and energy into new sites, new functionalities. You had to financially exploit the digital environment but no one knew how. You had to publish digital media and we did that as profusely as possible, in a mad rush to lock-in visitors through as many clicks and polls as possible.

But these investments did not produce the desired result: that is, an increase in subscription sales.

NRC Handelsblad could see that, compared to the other newspapers in the PCM group, its readership was ageing more rapidly. 'It was long held that students gravitated to *De Volkskrant*, and when people got a little more advanced in their careers and saw that the management was reading the *NRC Handelsblad*, they would switch', according to Jensma:

> I was a young editor-in-chief. I was 38 and the core staff at the paper was also young or quickly becoming younger. We could see that the group we belonged to, and the one coming up behind us, that it was totally absent from the picture and did not feel at all drawn to *NRC Handelsblad*. In marketing terms, the brand image of *NRC Handelsblad* was vague for this group or even completely non-existent.

Research showed that young, well-educated people viewed the *NRC Handelsblad* as the best newspaper in the Netherlands but did not choose it for themselves. The paper had no relevance or meaning for this target group. At the same time, the reading time for the newspaper was decreasing: people read it more selectively and were less able to obtain pertinent information out of it.

These two facts – the lack of connection with the young demographic and ever-shrinking amount of time people had to read a newspaper – raised the question of how *NRC Handelsblad* could attract young people. Jensma points out:

> We tried at that time, for example, to become involved in education. We set up a 'study house' website. The study house concept was an educational advancement at the time [not a physical space but an online environment for independent study] and we thought we could turn the newspaper content into a teaching tool and get a foot in the door that way.

Other attempts involved offering student subscriptions to *NRC Handelsblad*, but some in the PCM Group objected to offering a premium-priced product at reduced prices for a particular target group. 'We were absolutely tied to that price. I just couldn't mess with that. So, if I wanted to have something for the youth market, then I had to create something else. That was the condition', Jensma says.

That non-negotiable condition resulted in a weekly student edition based on the weekly foreign edition that already existed. Around the millennium, they published several pilot editions, which amounted to smaller versions of the *NRC Handelsblad*. And even though the copy was taken directly from the main newspaper, the focus groups' response from the market survey was negative. 'They didn't believe it was the *NRC*', Jensma explains. 'And that was very interesting to hear because not a single letter of new copy had been written for it. We pulled articles from the *NRC* and laid them out differently in the paper'.

The experience with the student edition led, in turn, to the idea of starting a financial morning paper. The favourable economic conditions provided an excellent sales market. By simply expanding the daily economic section somewhat, they thought they might be able to steal a share of the business market that had always, to that point, been dominated by *Het Financieel Dagblad*. As an added benefit, the publication of a morning newspaper would boost the visibility of *NRC Handelsblad*. But this initiative too was shot down: the investment needed was too high and people in the PCM Group thought that was too risky.

From experimentation to innovation

On the one hand, *NRC Handelsblad* was being forced by PCM Uitgevers to achieve better results; on the other, the culture at the publishing group was proving risk-averse. In 2005, Jensma was finally given the green light. 'To a certain extent, you could say that the discussion about a morning edition had been made possible by the fact that we had failed that time with the student edition. If we hadn't been stuck that time, *nrc·next* would have never come about'. In hindsight, the rise of APAX in 2001 as a venture capitalist at PCM Uitgevers probably also influenced the eventual approval of the launch of a morning edition.

The starting point for the new morning edition was the student edition, which they used as a basis for experimenting, making zero issues. Jensma recalls:

> The idea was that it had to be truly different, because you're concerned, of course, about cannibalism. So, the distance between the morning and the afternoon had to be as great as possible. The afternoon is a broadsheet, so that meant the morning was a tabloid. The next question was: are we going to call that thing 'NRC' or not?

They decided to stick with the *NRC* name but to replace '*Handelsblad*' with '*next*'. That allowed them to create a new image, while at the same time harking back to the recognizability of the *NRC* brand as a way of increasing visibility. And, of course, the plan for *nrc·next* was to rely heavily on copy from *NRC Handelsblad*. Jensma concludes:

> On the one hand, we were telling the market, 'This is new'. On the other, we weren't concealing the fact that 70 per cent of it came from the content of the afternoon paper, and that it was still possible to present something new from pre-existent content at another time of day, in another form and in a modified form, and that that can be the innovation.

Jensma pulled together a project group that included Gijsbert van Es of the *NRC* and Willem Jan Makkinga of PCM Uitgevers, who worked together to develop the *nrc·next* formula, and Jan Paul van der Wijk, who was responsible for the design. Jensma's role was primarily to shelter the project, so that the rest of the team could focus on this extraordinary task. 'You've never in your life set up a new newspaper from top to bottom. You've never developed a new product: you just have no idea', he muses.

They were given one year's time by the Board of Directors to prove themselves: *nrc·next* as a product had to be on the market within six months. The pressure was enormous, but so was the team's motivation. Jensma recalls:

> What motivated me was the urgency of the very tough situation we were in. And that for us, if we didn't succeed in handing down the *NRC* brand to a new generation or a

new target group or a new market segment, then it would be over in 20 years' time. I didn't want to be the editor-in-chief who missed the boat at this critical juncture.

Jensma approached Hans Nijenhuis for the position of editor-in-chief at the new newspaper under development. At the time, Nijenhuis headed the International desk at the *Handelsblad*. With his experience as a correspondent in Moscow, he had breathed new life into the International section, with a fresh new look and sense of presentation. That made him, in Jensma's eyes, the best person to help launch nrc·next.

From the very beginning, Nijenhuis and Makkinga decided to hang out together and met at least once a week in the early days of the project to think about what kind of newspaper it should be. 'This close collaboration between commercial and editorial staff was absolutely unique in the newspaper world', Nijenhuis points out. Makkinga had a marketing and advertising background and was the one who came up with the idea of accentuating a special feature every day in the paper. 'For instance, on Mondays, you feature sports, on Tuesdays, personal finance, on Wednesdays its careers and so on'. The guiding principle was that it should make little difference for the reader whether such topics were covered on a daily or weekly basis, but it would be attractive for advertisers. And that is exactly how it worked out in practice. 'And damned if he wasn't right. On Tuesdays, Makkinga had bank ads in the paper and on Wednesdays, placement ads in the paper, and on Thursdays and Fridays, he had entertainment ads', says Nijenhuis.

Besides the initial idea of re-using copy from *NRC Handelsblad* and Makkinga's idea of introducing a special accent each day of the week, Nijenhuis's team had to find the best way of presenting the news. What kind of added value would *nrc·next* be able to provide readers versus *NRC Handelsblad*?

The earlier market research results had revealed that people were finding a growing number of ways throughout the day to get their news – and that people had less time than ever to read the paper. Nijenhuis saw both of these variables as opportunities on which to base the *nrc·next* concept. 'What we want to do is save the reader time, to help the reader understand', he explains:

> He hears about a judge's ruling in his car or wherever. How should he interpret that ruling? As a newspaper, you need to be able to look ahead. How do you do that? By saying, for example, 'The ruling in this case will be announced at ten o'clock: eight scenarios for the takeover battle in the wake of the judgement'. If you read that article and then hear the ruling, you know: oh, so it's that scenario. Then, you have a frame of reference for the ruling, for making sense of it.

The way the news was presented in *nrc·next* also had to be different from other daily papers. Pictures are used to support the accompanying news story, which allows you to use fewer words to say the same thing. What's more, a greater reliance on images is more in keeping with the preferences of the younger generation. Here, too, Nijenhuis saw an opportunity to approach the news from a new vantage point – more as a daily magazine and less as a newspaper – by, for instance, not blowing a family drama up big on the front page but burying it deeper in the paper and then engaging in a discussion with the readership: 'Should we have printed this all over the front page?' 'It gives you, as a reader, a chance to read along with us', says Nijenhuis. 'You learn something about the media. Media are very important and you think, "It's good that they do that"'.

Makkinga points out that in writing the business case he looked at the market in a different way, from the perspective of the target group: highly educated young people between the ages of 25 and 40, who have a need for news that is both relevant and meaningful to them. 'Based on that, we decided to focus our efforts on segmentation and differentiation with regard to the other newspapers', he says. 'And with that concept as our starting point, we eventually managed to win over this target group'. An added benefit of this approach, moreover, was that it avoided cannibalizing the subscribers of other papers published by PCM. The formula, then, could be summed up as 'Know more in less time' – but with the necessary quality. 'The rise of free newspapers at that time was certainly something to take into account', Makkinga concedes. 'Our motto was "Not gratis, but status". And there, too, we differentiated ourselves'.

They hired an outside firm to help them come up with a good name for this new paper. 'Out of the 500 names they came up with, it was Jensma who resolutely made the decision: *nrc·next*', recalls Makkinga. The use of the English word 'next' originally met with some resistance but Jensma was not to be deterred.

NRC 'Miffy'

Out of all these ideas, then, the concept for *nrc·next* eventually took shape. The people at *NRC Handelsblad* were quite sceptical of this development. In fact, the majority of the editors were opposed to the idea of *nrc·next*, in part because the necessity for it was not explicitly clear to them. 'The general feeling was that it would be better if all that money and energy were pumped into the afternoon paper', Jensma says.

There was also a fear that the new paper would be a sort of *NRC 'Miffy'*[1] – too simplistic and lacking in content, which could possibly damage the image of *NRC Handelsblad*. Nijenhuis emphasizes the importance of not underestimating the youth demographic in that regard. Moreover, the premise involved sticking to the copy, or at least the quality, of *NRC Handelsblad*. 'The *NRC* as a hallmark, you really need that. The *NRC Handelsblad* articles that we used were not any shorter, either. They were just cut into pieces and presented in a different way: better, by taking more advantage of the possibilities afforded by image and layout', Nijenhuis explains.

All that scepticism disappeared the minute the newspaper hit the stands. 'Colleagues of mine were approached by people on the schoolyard who'd say, "I read your piece. That was a good piece". "Oh, yeah, in the *Handelsblad*". "No, in *nrc·next*"', recalls Nijenhuis. 'And they saw it that way, too: my article looks much nicer here. The writers started to realize, "We get more readers that way". And that's what they really want'. And their fear of simplification also disappeared as soon as they saw that their pieces were being left intact but just presented differently.

A new editorial board

Once the concept had been pulled off, it was time to hire new people who would be charged with constructing *nrc·next*. Based on the projected circulation, they would need a team of 24 people total. That team needed to include both experienced staff from *NRC*, who knew how to put out a newspaper, and a group of newbies who would tackle the job with fresh eyes.

What's more, to avoid having people recruit themselves, it was decided that this process, too, needed to be unlike the usual routine. That meant not taking on any interns; instead, they placed job announcements that included a very involved intake procedure. Nijenhuis says:

> Anyone interested had to fill out a form that would seriously take you about four hours to do well, because you had to write a news story and you had to write an essay and you had to tell all kinds of things about yourself, so any opportunists gave up immediately. We still received 700 forms.

Reading committees then got down to work reviewing those 700 candidates, looking explicitly for unusual details among the submissions. Nijenhuis recalls:

> There was one young woman whose hobby was Russia and she had a website in Russian. That's unusual; she is interesting. We had a young man who had a

column in *De Telegraaf*, but he also sometimes wrote for *De Groene Amsterdammer* [a journal of opinion] and he had studied philosophy. He is interesting. Different sorts. There was a young man who had written a book about house music or dance music and was an intern at the Ministry of Foreign Affairs. Interesting. We had this very large group of young people who were different from the usual group of *NRC* journalists. It was very important to us that they fill in the areas that we were missing.

In the end, 20 new young people were hired, with diverse and unusual backgrounds. The trick was going to be preventing them from assuming the corporate identity that prevailed at *NRC Handelsblad*. 'The greatest danger for people who come to work here is that they show up the next day in a suit and tie, that they suddenly start writing in a very serious tone, using lots of difficult words', says Nijenhuis. To prevent that from happening, he wanted a separate space in the building, where they could work on *nrc·next* with their new editorial team members. Unfortunately, because space was limited and the morning paper staff had different working hours than the evening paper staff – and so could easily share desk space – his request was denied.

When the new editorial staff was being given training on how to use the editorial system, they decided to squat that space. 'The space was pretty lousy', Nijenhuis admits. 'All it had was a telephone, but for creating our own identity, it was perfect'. At the same time, the new members of the editorial team needed to become part of the process at *NRC*. The very fact that they were sharing copy meant that they needed to know what was going on with the *Handelsblad* editors. So, people were spending some of their time at the various department desks.

The run-up and the launch

The new team was installed on 1 January 2006 and they had to have their first issue ready for publication on 15 March 2006. In the ten weeks that remained, they worked fervently experimenting and running trials. 'We used January for training', says Nijenhuis, 'and after that, we would think up a cover every day – not really make it, but what would the topic be, how would we do things. Starting two weeks ahead of time, we would make up a real *next* and that would then actually be printed but not published'.

This series of trials was to make sure everything worked properly. Since the editorial team consisted of only 24 people, Nijenhuis had decided not to hire a secretary or appoint senior editors but to deploy all his resources on the newspaper's content and design. 'That was a huge mistake', he admits. 'It was full of errors. So, I went to Jensma and we got assistance from six additional people in no time – experienced people who worked at *Handelsblad* and came to help us with the spelling and punctuation. When it comes time to truly start, you have to have the flexibility to change gears quickly and redirect things, and that's when you need a manager who can help you'.

The first issue of *nrc·next* was scheduled to drop on 15 March 2006, but headstrong as they were, they started a day earlier. To build brand and product awareness as fast as possible, a confrontation and trial strategy was implemented. That was seen as crucial; *nrc·next* had to be as solid as a house from day one and it was therefore necessary to acquaint as many people in the target group as possible with the newspaper in the shortest period of time. That is why on 14 March 2006 approximately 500 000 free copies of *nrc·next* were sampled at various high-traffic target group locations, such as train stations, universities and festivals.

From that point on, things really took off. That headstrong nature that differentiated them from others also occasionally led to some missteps, such as failing to report on a large news event. Nijenhuis explains:

> I can still remember it. It was an earthquake in Indonesia that killed a lot of people. But earthquakes are always the same. So, you know what, we're not going to cover it. We'll do something else. Turns out, though, the reader sees the images of that earthquake and becomes emotionally involved with the earthquake, and he wants to read something about it in the paper. 'Why we're not interested in the earthquake' as an article, that could have been a way to go, but you have to have some link to what's happening.

The target for *nrc·next*'s first year was fairly ambitious at 32 000 subscribers: after only eight months, though, they already had over 38 000. Makkinga had launched a tough confrontation strategy: eight weeks of *nrc·next* for €8. And the advertisements were coming in nicely too; with the target group strategy (a different theme each day), advertising revenue was 50 per cent higher than originally budgeted. Thanks to this well-conceived media strategy, *nrc·next* started winning various advertising awards, too.

After a year and a half, it became time for Makkinga and Nijenhuis to reflect on where they were headed. What was the next step? They came up with the idea of revamping the entertainment and travel features into a lifestyle supplement. Nijenhuis drafted a journalistic strategy plan, in which he indicated that he would need four extra full-timers to carry out the plan. Makkinga provided the financial analysis. Together, they took their plan to the publisher of

NRC Handelsblad and the newly installed editor-in-chief, Jensma's successor. Staffing at certain of the *NRC Handelsblad* editorial desks was very tight at the time, however, which meant that the editor-in-chief was reluctant to hire four new people to further expand a 'lifestyle' feature. 'We argued that we had arranged it so that those four would easily pay for themselves and that we'd be able to expand it from there, but the answer was still no, unfortunately. That's when we first realized that being part of something bigger can also be a disadvantage in terms of innovating your own product', Nijenhuis points out.

Handelsblad and *next*: two peas in a pod?

In late 2007, when there was a downturn as a result of fewer advertisements and it came time to cut costs, there were some adjustments made to the *nrc·next* concept. For one thing, the cuts were distributed evenly across the two newspapers, even though *nrc·next* was still thriving. One of the adjustments involved the internal billing procedure for the cost of correspondents working on *NRC Handelsblad* articles, articles that were also published in *nrc·next*. Those internal charges boosted the profitability of *Handelsblad*, while negatively impacting that of *next*. 'We drove each other totally nuts with those calculation models. When you start having these people who should be going out onto the streets and doing fun things making these kinds of calculations, then you know it's game over', Nijenhuis bemoans.

In late 2008, Nijenhuis was offered another job, which he accepted. By that point, Makkinga, too, had left. PCM had since become De Persgroep and they put *NRC* up for sale. It was bought by the private equity firm Egeria and Derk Sauer. They brought Nijenhuis back to *NRC* as publisher and he used the opportunity to put things back in order internally. As of 1 January 2013 he is back in the editor-in-chief's seat at *nrc·next*, where he has restyled the paper. He says:

> What we've done recently is to take *next* back a bit to the old formula. Right now, we have a big recruitment campaign going, so we have to get all that settled, then we sit down and consider: can we take that next step – to eventually publish a Saturday edition? But the climate has changed, in the sense that newspapers are under even more pressure because of the economic crisis. It's different than it used to be.

Four operational elements in the venture process

Organizations use a variety of tactics to structure innovation. In the corporate world, more specifically, the technology industry, innovation in large organizations is generally set up by forming a separate department, the so-called venture unit. This department tends to operate independently but falls under the control of the parent company. The primary reason for situating the department off on its own is so that it can have the space and freedom to experiment, to take chances. In large organizations, with their sales targets that have to be met, a unit like that can run into problems fitting in. At the same time, the innovations achieved within the venture unit must at some point be able to be incorporated into the parent company's operations, since that was generally the reason behind investing in innovation development in the first place. That is not always easy because these new innovations (ventures) can sometimes start leading a life of their own, partly as a result of the freedom they have been given for development.

We will be taking a look at how the innovations at NRC evolved, based on the four operational elements. How did *NRC Handelsblad* set up the innovation? Did they refer to a specific model? Then, we will examine the strategic positioning of the innovations. To what degree was a portfolio perspective adopted? How were the teams formed? Were team members recruited based on certain competencies? If so, what competencies were required? Finally, we will examine the relationship between the parent company and the venture organization. How do these organizations relate to one another? Do the innovations feed into the parent company's strategic objectives?

Use of a model

The *NRC Handelsblad* case is unique from the perspective of corporate venturing. In this situation, the necessity to innovate did not lead to the formation of a separate department for developing innovations, but instead to various new products. They experimented with websites, blogs, special editions and the like. And they kept at it until they had a new product that took off. It was therefore not so much a matter of innovation that was consciously planned but of an insight born of necessity that grew into an innovation.

The procedure followed was not based on the application of any particular model, but indirectly, the process could be viewed as roughly coinciding with the so-called stage-gate model. The idea that a new product was needed (Stage 0) led to the investigation of the business idea: a separate morning edition, distinct from the existing evening paper (Stage 1). After several adaptations to the idea, the editor-in-chief at *NRC Handelsblad*, Jensma, was given the green light by the Board of Directors of PCM Uitgevers to proceed to the next phase: further development of the plan into a concrete product

(Stage 2). Following a successful pilot project (Stage 3), there was the launch and a period of growth and expansion (Stage 4). The exit of *nrc·next* as a venture (Stage 5) is not yet part of the plan because the two newspapers are linked together through their mutual use of copy.

Portfolio

A portfolio contains an overview of the field in which one hopes to operate from a strategic perspective; it presents a framework that provides insight into what kinds of initiatives might or might not align with the organization's strategy. In the *NRC Handelsblad* case, the management of PCM Uitgevers can be viewed as the organization that designated the strategic playing field at the time, thereby defining the portfolio. In the beginning the field was very limited because they would not publish a morning edition, did not want to print the paper in any other size and refused to allow different pricing. And the experimentation with websites did not offer any realistic alternatives for a newspaper. You could argue, however, that the strategic portfolio of PCM Uitgevers was aimed at disseminating the news through both paper and digital means. In that sense, *nrc·next* unfolded within the strategic portfolio. The portfolio has since widened, now that, for instance, debates are also being organized in the NRC restaurant; news is being carried further than just on paper and the internet.

Team composition

The people behind *nrc·next* were very deliberate and thorough in forming the team of new editors, in accordance with a process they determined ahead of time. They set clear criteria the new editors had to meet, in order to ensure that the objectives the innovation had to achieve could be realized. They also specifically took into account the fact that *nrc·next* did not operate on its own as a separate venture unit and so took care to avoid contamination from the corporate identity at the *Handelsblad*. They knew what they wanted: interesting young people, who had a fresh eye for the news and their own opinions and were engaged and headstrong.

Relationship to parent company NRC Handelsblad

As previously mentioned, this case differs from other cases on this point because NRC did not establish a separate venture unit for developing new innovations. The origins of *next* were not a consciously planned innovation but the result of adeptly mobilizing and channelling the creativity and drive to 'not just leave it at that' that existed within the organization.

The relationship between the *Handelsblad* and *next* evolved naturally, since the entire business model for *next* was founded on using copy from the *Handelsblad* (and vice versa: *Handelsblad* also uses copy from *next*). Although there were originally some internal doubts about the next initiative and a fear that it would not do justice to the content of the articles when re-publishing them (*NRC 'Miffy'*), everyone eventually realized, in hindsight, that the emergence of *next* definitely added value to NRC as a whole.

By explicitly choosing to form an editorial team consisting of journalists who were fundamentally different from the old guard (younger, free thinkers, different vision), Nijenhuis made sure he did not just create a second *Handelsblad* but instead an entirely new team. Because of the lack of space, overlap in working hours and similar needs on the journalists' part in terms of news information, the two editorial teams were 'forced' to work together during the implementation process, as a result of which the relationship in this area, too, evolved naturally. All in all, it has to be said that the connection between the *Handelsblad* and *next* was successfully achieved.

What's next?

Earlier this year, the *NRC* relocated from Rotterdam to Amsterdam. They moved into a gorgeous glass building, right in the middle of the city, with a restaurant downstairs. 'Being in this building allows us, as journalists, to look outside and see the news happening out there', says Nijenhuis. 'And since we are so centrally located, our columnists, like Youp van het Hek, deliver their copy in person, which means people on the street can see and talk to them'. The restaurant gives people a chance to further pursue the debates from the Opinion page live and in person, so that now the *NRC* is something you can not only read, but also experience. And that's how *NRC* keeps working on new ways of spreading the news.

NOTES

* This case study was made possible in part with the assistance of Liesbeth Brackel. As business operations manager, she was involved in the inception of *nrc·next* and jointly responsible for its success.
1 Miffy is the English translation of a Dutch character in the children's books *Nijntje* (Little Rabbit).

9

Discussion and conclusions

Jessica van den Bosch and Geert Duysters

For each and every organization that participated in our study, venturing was seen as a window to new opportunities. All felt that, as a large organization, they had difficulties in dealing with their turbulent, and often disruptive, environment. Corporate R&D departments take years to come up with innovations and generally have a hard time thinking outside the box. At Océ Canon, for instance, efforts were initially focused on the printer market, whereas the true innovations were found to be in a much broader or even completely different market.

Venturing offers these organizations an opportunity to create an entrepreneurial environment and allows them to more easily adopt innovations that have been developed by, often small, outside companies. Here, a distinction needs to be made between internal and external venturing. With internal venturing, a separate business unit is created within the organization that is charged with developing ideas that come from within the organization but tend to remain unexplored due to a lack of time or money. Examples of this sort of venturing are AkzoNobel's New Ventures and the InnovationLab at TU/e. External venturing involves allocating a specific budget or setting up a fund under a separate company business unit for investing in innovations being developed outside the organization: Unilever, Océ Canon and Sanoma all pursued this form of venturing. There is also a hybrid form known as cooperative venturing, in which a business unit at an organization will enter into a partnership with one or more external parties and work with them to develop and roll out a new business idea. That is how CbusineZ undertook its venturing activities.

There are two notable exceptions in this group: that is, *nrc·next* and Rabobank. The *nrc·next* platform emerged not so much as a product of venturing, but as a form of strategic entrepreneurship, innovation that strengthens the competitive position of the parent company. In this case, you could refer to it as sustained regeneration, tapping into a new target group (market) with an existing, but modified, product. It was not strictly 'venturing', since the company did not establish a separate business unit to further develop its internal ideas. Moreover, there was no fund established for investing in external business ideas that were thought to be consistent with the company's strategic ambitions, nor did they partner with outside parties.

The other exception is Rabobank. Stemming from its cooperative roots, the company decided not to erect some organized innovation business unit, but rather appoint a Strategy and Innovation team within the Product Management unit to actively seek out innovative external developments. The team is not a separate business unit and does not have its own budget, other than that required for FTE (full-time equivalent) salaries. That means that for every innovation they want to capitalize on, they must proceed through the extensive internal circuit to get to the end result, which generally takes the form of shared ownership. This form of innovation may seem related to external venturing, but in terms of how it is organized you could also argue that it is simply a case of a business division pursuing Merger & Acquisition. That is also, in our view, its weakness; the division lacks a well-defined position within the parent organization and therefore also the capacity for following or withstanding external developments. This form of innovation can also be coined 'strategic entrepreneurship' or, more particularly, 'organizational rejuvenation'. Internal processes and structures are adapted so that strategic objectives can be better implemented to strengthen competitiveness.

In order to distil best practices from our cases, we will have a look at the four key operational elements that we distinguished in the introduction.

Use of a model

As discussed throughout the book, organizations use models to manage their innovation processes. While these can be helpful for maintaining oversight and boosting efficiency, it is also important to preserve the freedom inherent to the entrepreneurial process. All of the organizations in our study used some version of the stage-gate model as an aid for achieving results. You will recall that each stage concludes with a decision being taken as to whether to proceed with the venture, possibly pouring more time and money into it, or terminate it.

The weakness of this stage-gate model is the fact that once you have invested in the venture, admission to subsequent stages makes it harder to kill the venture since the scope of the investment increases in each stage. This escalation of commitment could result in ventures being pushed onto the market (see, e.g., AkzoNobel's New Ventures case study). Another disadvantage is that when process management models are used, there is less room for experimentation. In his book *The Lean Startup* (2011), Eric Ries advocates the vision of applying the lean method to start-ups and ventures. He sees a venture as an experiment where you test the assumptions made in a business plan. As soon as the assumptions become facts, a minimally viable product should be built and implemented on a micro-scale but paid for by customers. That way the product can be adjusted to the needs of the customer through a continuous process of improvement.

A third disadvantage of the stage-gate model is that more transformational innovations are unsuitable for a funnel approach (Nagji and Tuff, 2012), since it is often difficult to predict the market results for a product that no one has experienced before. If subjected to the stage-gate process, these game-changing ideas might be killed before they even get the chance to emerge from the funnel. The use of stage-gate models can therefore lead to so-called 'false negatives', which refer to promising products or technologies that are killed too early.

Some of the organizations under study, such as CbusineZ and Océ Canon, stuck to the stage-gate model quite closely. They strictly met all the milestones and requirements for moving from one stage to the next. Others, such as AkzoNobel's New Ventures and the TU/e InnovationLab, relied less heavily on the model. Their experience was that the process of achieving innovation cannot necessarily always be governed by process structures and that, in fact, these can negatively impact the requisite creativity. Those who had deliberately chosen for a strict application of the model argued, on the other hand, that a tightly directed process model supports them in achieving the desired results within a realistic timespan. They contend that creativity is most essential at the idea stage and that the other stages in the model should be closely managed.

There is something to be said for each of these visions. Looking at the results attained, based on the outcomes in our limited study, you might propose that a tightly managed organization produces results more quickly. An organization such as Unilever Ventures, which operates like a management company that advises the parent company on what investments to make, might not specifically use the model themselves, but they will appoint a person from the venture organization as part of the venture team to keep an eye on things. As Managing Director John Coombs put it so nicely, 'If every time one of our companies missed its targets, we killed it, we would have nothing left in that portfolio. Every single one we would have killed'.

When it launched *nrc·next*, *NRC Handelsblad* did not follow any specific model, but in hindsight you can identify each of the stage gates in the formation process. Although there seemed to be a lot of resistance from headquarters (PCM Uitgevers), they continued pursuing the idea that formed the basis of *nrc·next* anyway. This shows that early resistance should not always lead to the termination of a project. If they would have been strict and killed the venture early, this would have been a typical example of a false negative, in which a venture that could have proved successful was terminated.

Striking a balance between ditching a disappointing venture early on and not being afraid to 'kill your darlings' can be tricky. It is difficult to provide any general advice on this issue, which leads us to the main risk of venturing: the earlier the point in the process, the greater the uncertainty. That is one of the reasons Sanoma decided to invest in start-ups that were already up and running and had their first customers. This allows them to rule out some of the uncertainty since the business idea has already been proven. The downside of that is that the financial input needed at that point is greater than for a venture that has not yet hit the market. You might then, as a venture organization, want to balance the number of early start-ups and established start-ups in your portfolio to spread the risk and success rates.

By creating a balance between planning on the one hand (through the stage-gate model) and experimenting, as proposed by Ries, you can focus on the process as well as the outcome of the product, which generally leads to better and more innovative venture results.

Portfolio

As soon as a company has created a shared vision on how innovation will aid in realizing growth and competitiveness, it needs to come up with a plan for action. What strategic topics are relevant for the future? How much time and money needs to be invested to realize these strategic ambitions? How should the process be structured? All this information is key if a company wants to coordinate the process successfully.

By creating a portfolio, the company defines what strategic topics they envision to be relevant for the future. For example, SanomaVentures focuses on online consumer services, mobile and tablet apps, online video and connected TV, e-commerce, online advertising and marketing, and e-learning. Sanoma is one of the leading media and education companies in the Netherlands, providing information and entertainment in many European countries through various channels (e.g., TV, websites, events and apps).

They are also one of the largest publishers of magazines. Faced with the rise of web-based products on the one hand, and the financial crisis, which depressed sales of luxury goods such as magazines, on the other, they were forced to seek out alternative business models. So their focus on more web-based products is the result of the changing market environment and changing technological opportunities. By defining the six strategic topics listed above, they gave direction to their SanomaVentures innovation unit.

The same goes for CbusineZ, the venture organization of CZ, a large health care insurance company. They incorporated a strategic focus on enabling self-management within health care, quality improvement, cost reduction and availability of care. First, this focus implies that all ventures that are being created are related to at least one, but sometimes two or more, of these topics, thereby contributing to the parent company's strategic aims in the long run. Second, having insight into these portfolio themes also helps create a balance in the venture activities they undertake. If too many new ventures are focused on only one or two of the portfolio themes, they need to shift their focus to other, less-pursued issues to maintain a balance in their strategic aims. Third, by focusing on the portfolio themes, CbusineZ is able to put in place the right tools and capabilities for managing the ventures. As we will see from the cases, a well-balanced portfolio is key to providing corporate alignment, risk management and focus.

Most of the organizations in this study defined a portfolio to serve as a framework for the kinds of ventures they would be looking for. This generally meant seeking compatibility with the strategic domains defined by the parent company (e.g., Unilever) or with the strategic objectives upon which the very existence of the venture organization was founded (e.g., Document Services Valley as an innovation organization affiliated with Océ Canon). Two of the organizations did not, however, specifically manage their venture development by formulating a pre-defined portfolio.

The TU/e InnovationLab, for instance, does not have a portfolio but is inspired instead by interesting research developments. The multidisciplinary nature of the developments, however, is generally a key factor, as the company's Manager of New Business Development, Bart de Jong, points out. 'At the intersections where departments overlap, that's where the best things originate', he says. 'Not through monoculture, but an industrial designer working with someone from electrical engineering or someone from electrical engineering working with a chemist. Time and again, that's where the greatest ideas originate'.

AkzoNobel's New Ventures also did not have a strict portfolio policy; rather, the venture investments were determined much more by trends in the market that the business units risked losing out on otherwise. The new ventures organization at AkzoNobel being structured by Jos Keurentjes, Director of Technology and Open Innovation, has already defined a portfolio, the various areas of which reflect as a whole the strategic focus of the parent organization.

The advantage of a portfolio is that it provides orientation in terms of where you should be investing as a venture organization. The world is full of possibilities, but they are not all equally relevant to the parent organization's strategic future. By making conscious decisions, you introduce focus and it becomes easier to determine what you should invest in and what you should pass up. Of course, this is still no guarantee of success. The future is difficult to predict and certain ventures will turn out to be more or less relevant for the parent organization over time than they were thought to be initially. A venture portfolio can be compared to a portfolio of growth stocks in which you want to invest in a number of potentially important future products and technologies. An ideal portfolio includes risky, potentially new blockbusters, as well as projects that produce quick wins for the organization. Balancing the portfolio is key for the survival of the venturing units. Corporate management might lose interest in long-term investments. Quick wins generate successes and keep management's attention. Moreover, they facilitate a positive entrepreneurial spirit in the venture organization.

Team composition

Innovation units that have a clear cooperative venturing policy (see, e.g., the CbusineZ case study) need to make sure that they have the right people 'on board' and that these people team up with the right people from the external party with whom they want to create a joint venture. In cases where venturing is strictly internal (more an incubator activity), the people who come up with a great idea are probably the more entrepreneurial people within the company anyway. They need to get support from within the organization in order to realize and grow their idea and prevent it from being crushed by the parent company's bureaucracy.

All of the venture organizations have 'certain kind of people' on their staff. The descriptions given when they were asked about their team composition included 'builders', 'go-getters', 'entrepreneurial people' and 'free thinkers'. Some organizations explicitly chose to bring in outside people who would view things with new eyes (NRC); in others it was the mavericks with an entrepreneurial spirit who found their way to the venture organizations (AkzoNobel, Océ Canon, Sanoma). But everyone agrees on the fact that venturing requires people with a particular attitude and mindset.

Not only is the level of involvement and commitment on the part of the venture managers essential to the success or failure of the ventures, but also to a great extent their knowledge and skills dictate how the process will evolve. You might recall that the Psy Health Direct venture at CbusineZ was completely ready to go to market and yet the directors were unable to make it happen. When it became clear that it was the dynamics between the two directors that was preventing the venture from getting past the business plan stage, the solution was simple; with the appointment of a new director, the process was set back in motion and Psy Health Direct was eventually launched successfully.

The composition of the venture team is equally important. All of the organizations named diversity among team members as a critical factor. A combination of extraverted and introverted people, business-minded people and financial experts, lawyers and coaches, journalists and sales professionals and so on, creates the conditions for success at a start-up. By assembling a multidisciplinary team, you bring together the broad range of knowledge and expertise that will be needed at various points in the venture process and can then also be deployed.

Finally, in external venturing projects the cooperation between the venture team and the start-up is critical. The two parties have generally come together because they each have something to offer the other, but that is not always a recipe for success. Sometimes the start-up ends up wanting to (or does) head in another direction than originally envisioned. In such cases, dissolving the partnership is the only solution, whereupon the start-up can seek another partner if it wants. Similarly, in cooperative venturing, strong relations between the corporate and the external partner are essential to a successful partnership; the mere fact of entering into a joint venture is no guarantee for a happy marriage. The venture can only grow if it benefits, and continues to benefit, both parties. The moment the underpinnings of that partnership disappear, the venture's reason for existing ceases to be.

Relationship to the parent company

The relation between a venture unit and its parent company is of importance specifically at two moments during the process: when the venture organization starts and when a venture needs to be integrated. When a corporate decides to start with venturing, it needs to be aware of the fact that venture units need a certain amount of freedom to be entrepreneurial. The bureaucracy of the parent company often impedes a venture unit from realizing its goals because the venture needs flexibility and not efficiency to live by. On the other hand, when a venture unit successfully realizes a product or technology that is of value to the parent company, there comes a time when that venture needs to be integrated into the parent company ('spun in'). In order to integrate successfully, venture directors need to think about how they will eventually organize the integration long before it is actually going to happen.

As previously mentioned, the strategic objective for medium-sized and large organizations in venturing is to take out a kind of option on future developments. By investing in new ideas and young companies, the corporates hope to keep up with the latest trends and developments, which occur ever more rapidly, such that even their R&D departments cannot always keep up. The fact that the chief motivation for investing in venturing tends to be a company's strategic objectives and not financial incentives (it is not a money-earning exercise for any of the organizations, as it is for venture capitalists) means that in almost every instance the knowledge and expertise gained through the venturing experience must eventually 'land' somewhere in the parent organization. However, venture organizations are often positioned at arm's length from the parent organization. (Their entrepreneurial activity requires a certain level of freedom.) That can make it tricky to avoid having everything they develop viewed as non-essential by the employees at the parent organization because it is not a core business: the 'not invented here' syndrome.

To prevent the innovations from being kept at arm's length after they are developed, you need to have a strategy and plan in place before those new ideas are developed, which facilitates smooth coordination between the venture and the parent organization. The most obvious method for this is to involve people from the parent organization in the venture from the very start. This can be done in a number of ways: by having them participate in brainstorming sessions (CbusineZ); by appointing people from an appropriate business unit to serve as coaches or advisors for the venture (Sanoma); or by appointing people to work part-time as the venture manager, while retaining their position at the parent organization part-time (AkzoNobel's New Ventures).

At NRC that coordination was achieved by having *NRC Handelsblad* and *nrc·next* share and exchange copy, which allowed the two papers to benefit from each other's work. And at the TU/e InnovationLab the focus with regard to start-ups is not on spin-ins (i.e., integrating the business into the parent organization) but on spinning out the technology for the ultimate purpose of creating an ecosystem that will, over the long term, result in more investment in research. Another company where integration was not the premise is Unilever Ventures. They operate more like a venture fund that invests in markets of interest to Unilever. If a self-reliant business results from that, more so the better; it does not necessarily have to be integrated into Unilever.

Document Services Valley was financed by Océ Canon as a way to gain insight into new technological developments that were relevant to the company, but it is not officially a venture organization. In the meantime the possibilities DSV affords are becoming clear and the company is looking into how they could use it as a model for the camera market. With its new ventures model, AkzoNobel has decided to assume the position of a launching customer for start-ups, which should also help accelerate the process of attracting interest from venture capitalists. This allows the parent organization to be adequately involved in further developing and expanding the start-ups, without having to provide the investment capital, thereby limiting the financial risk.

All of these practical solutions have proven easier said than done when they were being implemented. The fact remains that when a venture is ripe for integration into the parent company, a host of issues comes into play. One is size: ventures are frequently relatively small compared to the business unit they wind up in. This puts the venture at risk of being crushed by the core business: its smaller size means it receives less time, money and attention, causing the innovative product or service to die a slow death. Another danger is that of cultural differences between the venture and the parent company. People at the venture are accustomed to having the freedom to tackle matters in an enterprising fashion. When a venture is forced to adopt the procedures of its parent organization, which are usually more bureaucratic, this generally produces a culture clash. The question then is whether or not you should integrate a venture into the parent company and, if the answer is yes, when the appropriate time for doing so is. This will inevitably take some serious deliberation.

10

Top ten best practices for managing corporate ventures

Jessica van den Bosch and Geert Duysters

Despite the difficulties associated with the creation and management of corporate ventures, most of the organizations studied considered them key to their long-term survival. Corporate venturing allows them to catch up with new developments, enables them to reposition themselves and creates a window to new opportunities. It is vital for creating an ambidextrous organization that is efficient in terms of running its core business, while at the same time keeping an eye on future developments.

Regardless of the vast differences in our cases in terms of technologies and sectors, we can identify many commonalities in terms of practices that seem to generate the best results. In an effort to distil the most important best practices, we have carefully analysed the cases and performed additional interviews with key stakeholders in the ventures. This investigation has led to some surprising, but robust, findings, which we outline below.

1   Team, team, team

Realtors like to say, 'Location, location, location'. We say, 'Team, team, team'. Some organizations only assign people to venturing units who they can spare at their headquarters, whereas a venture needs the best people in the organization, people with entrepreneurial spirit who are willing to take risks, can work on a multidisciplinary team and are intensely passionate about the product or technology they are working on. A venturing team should consist of not only engineers, but also people with a clear business sense who are willing to bring a new product or technology to the market. The people in the team should not have a vested interest in the parent organization, although good contact with headquarters or business units is key.

2 Physical/organizational separation

The most successful venturing organizations are physically, mentally and organizationally separated from the main organization. At the same time these organizations are able to benefit from synergies of branding, customer/ supplier networks, technological know-how and financial resources with the parent company. This proves to be a delicate balance; units kept at arm's length can suffer from a lack of synergies, while closely integrated units might lack the necessary entrepreneurial culture that is typical of highly successful ventures.

3 Alignment and top management commitment

Despite the above-mentioned entrepreneurial spirit that has to be created, ventures need to be aware of aligning with corporate agendas. In general, headquarters will lose interest in a venture once there is a certain degree of strategic misalignment. While at the start of a venture, alignment is often secure, the agendas of a company's top management are likely to change over time. Venture managers should be aware of these changes and periodically assess whether they are still contributing to the overall corporate agenda. Once you lose the management's commitment, it will be extremely difficult to secure funds, benefit from corporate synergies and survive in the long run.

4 Building a healthy portfolio

As in a stock-market portfolio, you need to find a balance between risk and rewards. At the beginning it is important not to be overly ambitious and to be able to generate a few quick wins, which provide energy and a positive mindset for the people in the venture and corporate management. It is important to measure, communicate and celebrate successes. Organizations should realize that ventures are risky and that the majority of them do not lead to financial success. Even failures, though, often generate interesting knowledge for the organization about future directions. Finding out that a certain direction is not technologically feasible can protect firms from spending large amounts of R&D funds on related projects. Also market information can be enhanced through ventures. Overall, there is increasing consensus that ventures enhance the survival chances of organizations in the long run and might generate new blockbusters for firms. Finally, the portfolio should reflect the future direction the firm envisions.

5 Benefiting from partnerships

There is enormous value in partnerships. Partnerships allow you to 'cherry pick' from the best available sources worldwide. Collaboration with competent partners enables cost and risk sharing and technological learning, reduces time-to-market and facilitates creativity through the combination of different ideas. Furthermore it aids in sharpening the business case. Working with external partners requires you to prove the credibility of your assumptions and helps you to remain critical.

6 Performance rewards and bonuses tied to goals

Most organizations are hesitant to treat venture unit employees differently from their corporate employees. However, rewards should always be tied to goals. If your goal is to create an entrepreneurial unit, you should aim to reward successes and not punish failures. The use of stock benefits/ownership attracts and motivates entrepreneurial people in a much better way than regular financial arrangements. In similar vein, it is important that venture managers who have led a 'failing' venture not be seen as losers but heralded as entrepreneurs and passionate people.

7 Speed is king

The most successful ventures are often the ones that act swiftly. Any form of bureaucracy can kill a venture. Venturing is all about ideas, speed and execution. These should be recognized as key success factors by top management and the venturing team. Lean start-up methods often prove to be successful in venturing organizations.

8 Use of stage-gate processes

The most successful organizations make use of clear milestones and stage-gate processes. These stage-gate processes provide clear guidelines for venture management and enable swift decision-making. They also prevent organizations from escalating commitment to ventures that have no future. Although some people would argue that such processes are bureaucratic and time-consuming, experience has shown that they can actually significantly improve the time-to-market for a new product or technology. Furthermore they facilitate the 'fail often, fail early, fail cheap' principle that is key to successful venturing processes.

9   Think small, act big

Small is beautiful in venturing. Small teams are often more committed, passionate and entrepreneurial. Small teams often act big in terms of developing new breakthrough ideas and products. Especially in the early phase of a project, there is no need to involve too many people. You can partner, outsource and even crowd-source your way into a new business. There is no need to create a large organization for the successful development of a project. Big ideas require small teams.

10   Capture your experiences

Venture management is a relatively new and unexplored field of business. Experience in most firms is limited and best practices are not readily available. Venturing is a balancing act; firms must continuously balance such aspects as entrepreneurship and efficiency, corporate goals and venture goals, separation benefits and synergetic effects, and so forth. Although this would seem impossible, there are some organizations that consistently outperform others in terms of venturing performance because they have captured experiences, learned about venturing and developed routines in their organizations that facilitate optimal execution of venturing processes. Therefore it is key to not only learn from others and from your own experiences, but also capture these lessons and develop them into routines and management practices.

References

Birkinshaw, J. and A. Campbell (2004, 9 August), 'Know the limits of corporate venturing', *Financial Times*.

Chesbrough, H. (2003), *Open Innovation: The New Imperative for Creating and Profiting from Technology*, Boston, MA: Harvard Business School Press.

Lerner, J. (2013, October), 'Corporate venturing', *Harvard Business Review*, pp. 86–94.

Nagji, B. and G. Tuff (2012, May), 'Managing your innovation portfolio', *Harvard Business Review*, pp. 66–74.

Osterwalder, A. and Y. Pigneur (2010), *Business Model Generation*, Hoboken, NJ: Wiley.

Ries, E. (2011), *The Lean Startup*, Harlow, UK: Pearson.

Schumpeter, J.A. (1939), *Business Cycles*, New York: McGraw Hill.

Index